I AM JESUS OF NAZARETH: THIS IS MY STORY

AS TOLD BY LORD JESUS CHRIST IN COLLABORATION WITH

MYRA LOPEZ

ISBN: 979-8-9992201-0-3

To order additional copies of this book, contact:
lizarnews@gmail.com

DEDICATION

To the one reading this book. If you feel lost, the world doesn't make sense right now, and perhaps you're not even sure why you picked up this book, I get it. Life can knock the wind out of us, twist our sense of direction, and make us wonder if we'll ever feel whole again.

I wrote this not as someone who has it all figured out but as someone who's wrestled with the same questions. If you're stumbling, doubting, or just tired of pretending to be okay, I hope these pages meet you where you are. I hope they remind you that it's not too late to turn around, start again, and believe that healing and truth are possible. This book is my hand reaching out to yours. You're not alone.

This book was written with you in mind—with honesty, hope, and the belief that, no matter how far off course you feel, there is a way back. We're all trying to make sense of this world, especially in times like these. I want you to know that there's a better path that starts with faith. If these words help you take even one small step toward peace, then every page is worth writing.

TABLE OF CONTENTS

INTRODUCTION

— • • ● • • —

Writing this book didn't come about by design or by chance. It never would have occurred to me to write a Christian book. I've read parts of the Bible, but I'm certainly no Biblical authority. Something emerged spontaneously that led to this book's writing that I would never have imagined or anticipated. It happened just four weeks ago on a quiet morning. God awakened something deep within me that changed my life forever.

It was a Saturday morning, about 9:00 a.m. I was sitting at my computer editing a different book, as I had done many times before. In the stillness of that moment, I heard a clear and firm voice say to me, "Write my book." Astonished, I stopped what I was doing and, before I could react, the voice spoke again: "Write my story." There was a pause and then I heard the voice again say, "I am Jesus of Nazareth."

I froze, unable to move or understand what was happening. I began to cry and couldn't stop. Tears streamed down my face. I felt my heart pounding very hard. Was Jesus speaking to me? I wondered. I didn't know what to do or say. I felt confused. That's when I realized I had received a call from God. It wasn't my imagination; it was Jesus' voice, a request coming from heaven. From that moment on, I understood that my life could no longer continue as it was. I had a duty to convey a message that was not mine but Jesus'.

I didn't know that much about the Bible. I had read parts of it but not all. How could I write a book about Jesus without knowing His teachings? I began to pray and initiated a dialog with Jesus. I asked Him for wisdom and understanding so I could write His book. I prayed for His help. How would I do it?

I began writing, listening for Jesus' guidance as I worked. After twelve hours sitting in front of the computer, I finished the book. While writing it, I cried a lot. Jesus' words touched my heart like a sword piercing it. I didn't write this book, at least by myself. Jesus of Nazareth wrote the book through me.

This book is for anyone who wants to grasp the value of conversion and repentance in Christian life. Through these pages, you will discover Jesus' teachings on the fundamental Christian principles. You will find the testimonies within the Scriptures and reflect on the urgent need to be spiritually prepared for His return.

Jesus calls us to live holy lives, free from sin and committed to the truth contained within the Gospel. But losing sight of the path that leads us to eternal life is easy in a world of distractions. This book is not about theory. It is an invitation to transform our lives. Each chapter challenges our beliefs. It teaches us to reflect on our lives and shortcomings and everything we have done, both positive and negative. It teaches us to make decisions that will define our lives forever.

It invites us to a genuine, not superficial, conversion; to a complete renewal of mind and heart.

This book explores our relationship with God and outlines the path to a whole life. I pray that every word here touches the hearts of the readers. We must sincerely surrender ourselves to God.

May the Holy Spirit guide all your thoughts and may this message from Lord Jesus Christ be a light in the darkness.

May this book awaken minds, boost faith, and spark true repentance in everyone who reads it.

May this message from Jesus transform your life, as it transformed mine, with faith and humility.

CHAPTER 1

THE HOPE OF
A PEOPLE

For years, my people have waited for their Savior. He will fulfill my Father's promises. Since the days of Abraham, God promised to create a great nation from his descendants. Moses obeyed my Father and freed them from slavery in Egypt. He guided them to the Promised Land. During David's reign, Jerusalem shone with the glory of a lasting kingdom. After centuries of exile and suffering, Israel's hope became a deep longing.

I was born into waiting in times of oppression and hopelessness. I did not arrive in a time of peace. I came when my people lived under Roman rule. This foreign power imposed heavy taxes and had soldiers patrolling every street. I saw my people's suffering, their anguish, and their hopelessness. I saw their hearts cry out for a Savior. They wanted someone to free them, restore Israel, and fulfill God's old promises.

I remember the stories my mother told me. She shared how the angel announced my arrival. My birth was humble, in a manger, far from kings' palaces. My mother said shepherds came to see me, led by a vision. Wise men from the East also brought gifts. They knew I was the king they had waited for.

I grew up in Nazareth, a small and unimportant town. There, I learned a trade from my Father, Joseph. Wood became a part of my life: the smoothness of the shavings, the weight of the planks, the sound of the hammer. Every day, amid work, I observed my people. I saw the fatigue on their faces, the struggle to survive. I also noticed how they clung to the Law of Moses. They were seeking in it the answer to their suffering. I saw the Pharisees push for purity and obedience. The Sadducees held power in the temple through politics. The Zealots raised their weapons in rebellion.

Meanwhile, the Essenes retreated to the desert, awaiting God's judgment. Each one, in their way, sought redemption. But I knew salvation would not come through wars, rules, or isolation.

From a very young age, I felt the Father's call within me. When I was only twelve years old, I went with my parents to Jerusalem and stayed in the temple. There, I spoke with the teachers of the Law, asked them questions and answered theirs. I astonished them with my words, but it felt natural to me. I felt at home in my Father's house. But it was not yet my time. I returned to Nazareth and grew in wisdom and stature, awaiting God's appointed time.

The people were still waiting for a king. Many believed the Messiah would arrive with an army and a sword. They thought He would defeat Rome and set up a glorious throne in Jerusalem. But the Kingdom I brought was not of this world. It was not a kingdom of earthly power. I focused on transforming the heart. I did not come to free Israel from Rome's rule. I came to free the world from the dominion of sin and death.

When the time came, I knew I must begin my journey. God guided me to the Jordan River, where my cousin John was preaching and baptizing. People came to him because he spoke the truth and they trusted him. After all, he told them to prepare themselves, that the Kingdom of God was near. When I entered the water and John saw me, I knew he understood who I was. At first, he didn't want to baptize me; he said I should baptize him. But I insisted because I had to complete it all.

When I emerged from the water, heaven opened and the Spirit of God descended upon me like a dove. A clear, firm voice resounded: "This is my beloved Son, in whom I am well pleased." At that moment, I knew that the time had come.

From that day on, I marked my path. But it wouldn't be easy. Not everyone would accept what I came to bring. Some, even from my group, would turn away from my message. It didn't match what they expected. They wanted a political liberator, a warrior, a new David. I came to offer them something more: the Father's love, reconciliation, and the forgiveness of sins.

I can still see their faces: the priests in the temple, holding on to power; the Pharisees, focused on the Law but missing God's heart; the fishermen on the Sea of Galilee, worn out from work and wanting more; the women on society's edges and the joyful children playing close by.

I saw the poor fighting for food, the sick left alone, and the religious holding on to harsh rules. I saw the fear in the eyes of those who feared the empire and the longing of those who awaited the Messiah. They whispered about a king who would come with power, raise armies, and restore the Kingdom of Israel. But the Kingdom I brought was not of this world.

I did not come to condemn the world but to save it. My mission was not to set up a throne in Jerusalem but to open the way to the Father. I brought not chains or swords but freedom and life. Even though many didn't get it at first, I realized my journey would involve suffering and the cross. Still, I was sure my people's hope would not be in vain. Because God's love is greater than the power of men and that was the true promise I had come to fulfill.

I hadn't come to take a throne but to bring life, not to conquer nations but to conquer hearts. My Father sent me to give hope to the brokenhearted, heal the wounded, and seek and save those who are confused so they would not be lost. My people expected a liberator with a sword, but I came with love. I was sent to be an example of God's absolute, eternal love.

CHAPTER 2

THE BIRTH OF THE SAVIOR

M y story began long before that night in Bethlehem; my Father had prepared the way before He created the world. The prophets spoke of me, announcing my coming. They described the moment when light would descend upon the darkness. When the time came, I entered the world not as a king but as a fragile child born in humility.

My mother, Mary, was a simple young woman from Nazareth. She loved God deeply. So, when the angel Gabriel said she would give birth to the Son of God, she accepted it with faith. She didn't understand the full extent of what was happening.

My Father, Joseph, was a righteous man. At first, he doubted when he heard about my mother's pregnancy. Then God spoke to him in a dream and revealed that I had fulfilled the promise. Then, with love and obedience, he received me as his Son.

When my mother was pregnant, Emperor Caesar Augustus ordered a census. He wanted everyone to be counted. When my parents found out, they decided to leave Nazareth and go to Bethlehem, the city of David. The road was tough. With her swollen belly, my mother moved forward with patience and strength. When they arrived, the town was entirely full of travelers. There wasn't a single place to rest, so they found refuge in a stable at night. It was there that my mother gave birth to me. There were no royal announcements or palace trumpets, only the whisper of the wind and the comforting warmth of my mother's arms. She wrapped me in swaddling clothes and laid me in a manger, a simple animal feeding trough. At that moment, the glory of God shone not in golden temples but in the humility of a stable. Such was my first night on Earth.

But although my birth occurred in simplicity, heaven did not remain silent. In the nearby fields, a group of shepherds were tending their sheep. They were men forgotten by many and considered insignificant in society. Yet, they were the first to receive the news. An angel appeared to them in the night's darkness and God's glory surrounded them. With fear and awe, they heard the words that would change history: The voice told them not to be afraid. He also said he was bringing everyone good news and great joy. He told them that Mary would give birth to a boy named Jesus. " He will be the world's Savior, the Son of God.

With haste and without hesitation, the shepherds left everything and ran to find me. When they reached the stable and found me in the manger, they realized the impossible had come true. God's promise was being fulfilled before their very eyes. They worshipped with humility and, filled with joy, went to tell everyone what they had seen.

Several days later, other visitors arrived. They said a star in the sky guided them. They said they were wise men from distant lands who studied signs and knew all the ancient prophecies. They said they had seen my star shining in the east, so they followed it. They knew that the King, as promised by God, had been born.

As they entered the stable, they were moved; they bowed down and worshipped me. They didn't come by chance; my Father guided them. They brought me significant gifts, gold for my kingship, frankincense for my divinity, and myrrh to show that I would one day suffer and die for the world.

But not everyone received the news with joy. In Jerusalem, upon hearing of my birth, King Herod felt fearful. A new king meant a threat to his throne. Not understanding that my Kingdom was not of this world, he plotted to get rid of me before I could grow up.

God warned the wise men in dreams not to return to Herod and He also spoke to Joseph, telling him we must flee. In the middle of the night, we arose and left for Egypt, leaving the land of our ancestors behind. From my infancy, I faced rejection and persecution. Even as a child, the world was already trying to silence me. But my Father protected me.

After many years, we returned to Israel but not to Bethlehem. We went to Nazareth, where I grew up in a working-class family. In the eyes of the world, I was the carpenter's son. But deep down, I knew my mission was beginning.

My birth was not just an event in history. It was the fulfillment of an eternal promise. From my first cry in the manger to my last word on the cross, I had one purpose: to bring salvation, light, and hope to everyone who believes.

And so, in the humility of one night in Bethlehem, the Savior came into the world. From that moment in Bethlehem, my Father marked my life by His purpose. My birth was not a coincidence or a simple event in the history of Israel. It fulfilled a promise made long ago, back in Abraham's time. God said that his descendants would bless all nations.

The shepherds saw me and believed. The wise men sought me out and bowed down before me. But some feared my arrival; they saw in me a threat rather than a hope. It has always been this way. Some hearts open to the light, while others remain in the darkness.

My family and I lived as strangers in Egypt until the danger passed. When Herod died, my father, Joseph, received instructions to return to our homeland. Instead of going back to Bethlehem, we settled in Nazareth. It's a small town lacking in glory or importance.

There, I grew up, learned Joseph's trade, and lived among the ordinary people. At first glance, there was nothing special about me. But within me, my Father's voice resounded with clarity. I knew my time had not yet come, but every day, I drew closer to the mission for which He sent me.

The days of my childhood and youth were days of preparation. While the world continued to wait for its Messiah, I walked among them, unrecognized. But the time of my manifestation was drawing near. My people's hope was not in vain. The Savior was already here; soon, the world would learn the truth.

CHAPTER 3

CHILDHOOD AND YOUTH IN NAZARETH

———— · ·●· · ————

I grew up in Nazareth, a small and unimportant town in the eyes of the world. Its dusty streets, simple houses, and hardworking people were the setting for my early years. These were simple people who worked day after day to survive. The men worked the land or their fathers' trade while the women cared for their homes and taught their children.

I grew up surrounded by humble people: farmers who spoke of the hardship of work, fishermen who told their stories of the Sea of Galilee, and children who dreamed of a better future. I spent my childhood there, surrounded by familiar faces, neighbors who greeted each other daily and children who ran through the streets without a care.

From a young age, I felt drawn to the Scriptures. I focused on the Torah and the Prophet's readings in the synagogue. Every word spoke of my Father, His love, and His promises. As my companions learned the traditions of our ancestors, I understood that each prophecy pointed to my coming.

As the days lengthened and the seasons changed, my life in Nazareth continued calmly, marked by work and learning. There was nothing extraordinary about me in the eyes of the people who watched me grow, but there was something profound in my soul, something no one else could see. Others' eyes only saw a child and then a young man becoming a man, but something much more significant formed my spirit.

Even so, I lived like any young man in Nazareth. I helped at home, worked in the workshop with Joseph, walked through the fields, and observed the stars at night. No one in my village suspected I was the Messiah. To them, I was just Jesus, the carpenter's son.

My parents were always exemplary in their faith. My mother, always serene, reflected an unwavering trust in God. Maria told me stories about my birth, the shepherds who visited me, the wise men from the East who brought gifts, and how my family had to flee Egypt to protect me. I remember her loving gaze as she spoke to me about the voice of the angel, about

God's promise and how everything was written before I came into the world.

Every day, my mother taught me to pray, meditate on the Scriptures, and live in harmony with the will of our Creator. She was my first example of devotion and the love she showed me reflected my love for God.

My Father, Joseph, was a righteous and hardworking man. He taught me what it meant to be a man of integrity, humility, and hard work. Although I never had a direct relationship with my heavenly Father until much later, His love was evident in the care and dedication with which Joseph treated me. I spent hours in his workshop, shaping wood and building doors, tables, and plows for the villagers. From a young age, I spent time with him, watching him closely and learning the trade that had sustained our family. Wood became a part of my days: the smell of sawdust, the sound of the hammer, the feel of the wood chips in my hands.

But while my hands were learning to work with wood, my heart was elsewhere. From a young age, I felt a deep connection with my heavenly Father within me. Although I grew up like any other child, playing and learning in the synagogue, I felt that my purpose extended beyond what others could see.

I remember one day in particular that marked my childhood. I was twelve years old when my parents and I traveled to Jerusalem for Passover, as we did every year. It was a special celebration, one of the most important for our people. Pilgrims filled the city, the temple shone with brilliance overhead, and the aroma of sacrifices wafted through the air.

After the holidays, my family set out to return to Nazareth with a group of travelers. My parents thought I was with them in the crowd, but they became anxious when night fell and they realized I was gone.

They returned to Jerusalem and searched for me for three days. They found me in the temple. I was in the church, talking to the priests, listening to them, asking and answering questions. The elders stared at me in amazement, marveling at my understanding and answers. When my mother saw me, she ran to me, relieved but worried.

"Son, why have you done this to us? Your Father and I have been searching for you in anguish."

I replied with care, knowing my words might not make sense right then. "Did you not know I must be about my Father's business?"

They didn't fully understand what I said, but my mother had treasured those words. That day, although I returned with them to Nazareth and continued to grow in obedience, my soul knew that the time of my mission was approaching.

The years passed and my people's longing continued to grow. I listened to the conversations of the elders, the whispers of the priests, the expectations of the Pharisees, and the suffering of the poor. Everyone awaited the Messiah, but few imagined how He would come.

Some dreamed of a military leader who would free Israel from Roman rule. Others hoped for a high priest who would restore the people's purity. Little did they know that the Savior they awaited was not of this world, that the world's Savior would not come to fight or raise armies. Nor was he interested in taking the throne of Jerusalem by force. My mission was greater: to bring salvation, restoration, and eternal life.

From a young age, I knew I wasn't like other children. I felt different. I began understanding who I was and why I was here as I grew older. I often felt the need to speak and tell the truth. I wanted to tell them who I was, but it wasn't the right time. I had to wait for my Father's voice; He would let me know when the time came.

As I grew up, I listened to my Father's voice. I heard that voice increasingly clear in my heart. On nights in Nazareth, I looked up at the sky. I spent long hours gazing at the stars. I felt a sense of joy. I felt my Father's presence. His love and plan were slowly unfolding.

Every night, I meditated in silence, thinking about my future. I knew my life wouldn't be easy; I wasn't a simple man from Nazareth. I was there to do my Father's will. However, the right time had not yet arrived. The desire to follow the ways of my heavenly Father and fulfill His will burned in my heart, but the right moment had not yet arrived.

Even though everyone in Nazareth hoped for the Messiah, nobody saw me as the one to fulfill that promise. To them, I was the son of Joseph, a young worker who could one day take over his father's workshop. I did not feel distant from them or superior. On the contrary, I lived in communion with the ordinary people and shared their joys and sorrows. I helped however I could, from carpentry work to escorting the little ones to the synagogue.

I wasn't formed only in the synagogue. I also grew in moments of silence, prayer, and deep meditation. My soul yearned for more. I wanted to understand not only the words of the Torah but also the reality behind them. I felt my Father had called me to something great. I kept this in my heart, waiting for the moment to be revealed.

At times, I felt my life drifting away in a town that seemed unaware of the bright future ahead. Some looked at me with respect for my skill with my hands, but no one seemed to notice the flame burning within me. As I walked down the street, I noticed the people around me. I could see their daily struggles and the weight of their dashed hopes. There was suffering around every corner, and that, too, was etched in my soul.

Since I was young, the words of the prophets lived inside me. They weren't just lessons or stories—they felt like something I had always known as if they were written on my heart long before I could understand them. They spoke of a promised one who would bring sight to the blind, hope to the broken, and freedom to those in chains. Every time I heard their words, something deep within me stirred. It was as if they were speaking about me. And though I didn't fully grasp it then, I could feel the weight of it pressing on my soul—both a calling and a burden I could not ignore.

No one around me knew what I carried. To them, I was just Jesus—Joseph's son, Mary's boy. We played in the streets, shared meals, and laughed under the stars. But inside me, a storm was growing. I felt the call like fire in my bones but held it quietly. I wanted to cry out and tell them who I was and why I had come, but the time hadn't come yet.

I would watch the people—my neighbors, my friends, even strangers in the marketplace—and wonder if they could feel it too—that something was coming, that the world was about to change. I longed to speak, to reveal what the Father had placed within me. But I knew that revelation had its hour and mine had not yet come.

In Nazareth, they saw a carpenter, not a King; a helper in the shop, not the Hope of Israel. Still, I loved them. Even in their doubt, even in their blindness, I loved them. I waited with patience, though my spirit burned with the truth. Every day, I walked among them, knowing who I was and knowing most would never understand.

But I trusted my Father's timing. I trusted that, when the hour came, He would open the door. Until then, I listened. I learned. I watched the world with open eyes and an open heart. And I waited not as a distant Savior but as a son, walking the earth with the weight of heaven stirring inside me.

I wondered how people would react when they learned who I was. Would they believe me? Would they reject me? I knew it wouldn't be easy. I knew my path would lead me to sacrifice and face opposition and even those closest to me would doubt me. But there was no fear in my heart from the day I was placed in a manger until I would hang on a cross and bring salvation to the world.

As the years passed, I knew the wait was almost over. Soon, the silence of my youth would give way to the voice crying in the wilderness. Soon, the days of labor in the workshop would be behind me, and the sick, the sinners, and the broken would come to me seeking healing and forgiveness. Nazareth was my home, where I grew up and prepared myself. But my journey didn't end there. The entire world was to hear my Father's message. And so, with each passing day, prayer offered in secret, and word of Scripture pondered in my heart, the time of my mission drew near.

They didn't know it and they didn't understand it yet. Soon, the carpenter's son from Nazareth would walk among them.

They would finally see the hope they had held for centuries for a better life.

One day, as I walked through the hills around Nazareth, looking out over the peaceful landscape of Galilee, I felt a profound peace, as if creation itself were speaking to me. At that moment, the entire universe seemed to align and I understood that my mission was for my people and the world. The time prepared me for the work my heavenly Father had for me.

Despite all my reflections and dreams, my daily life continued as usual. The routine of work, prayer, and Torah study continued, but I knew deep within me that my life would soon change forever. The calling I had felt since I was young was now more apparent than ever and God's Spirit was preparing me for the path I was to take.

I knew it wouldn't be easy. The difficulties would be great, but the challenges would be even more significant. Sometimes, I doubted how people would react, whether they would genuinely accept me, whether they could see in me the promised Messiah. But it didn't matter because my Father's love was sufficient. In Nazareth, life seemed simple, peaceful, and familiar, but something more significant was brewing inside me. Soon, the stillness of those years would give way to a mission that would change history forever.

CHAPTER 4

BAPTISM AND THE DIVINE CALL

· • ● • · ——

T he day everything changed, my mission took shape before everyone's eyes and it was not like any other. I remember that day with a clarity that never fades. It marked the beginning of a path that would take me through the desert, toward the multitudes, and finally to the cross.

I grew up knowing the Scriptures, learning the Law of Moses, the prophecies of Isaiah, and the promises given to us, the people of Israel. Everything seemed to prepare me for something great, but I knew something was beyond human understanding. I knew that the Kingdom of God was not just a promise for my people but for the entire world. For years, I kept silent about that inner call, waiting for the moment my Father had shown.

It was then, when the Jordan River crossed my path, that everything became clear. I knew the time had come for me to make my appearance. I knew my ministry must start in that river, in the waters of purification my people had long awaited.

I had heard of John the Baptist, who preached repentance and the forgiveness of sins. His message touched many who went to the river for baptism. They felt their need for forgiveness and a fresh start. Some saw him as the forerunner of the Messiah, the one who would prepare the way for the Savior.

I knew in my heart that it was at that moment that my Father was calling me to emerge from the shadows of Nazareth and present myself to the world as the Son of God, as the one who would bring salvation.

The Jordan River was a place of encounter, reconciliation, and hope. Those who approached the water did so in search of something more profound. They didn't come just for a ritual but a true transformation of their hearts. In their eyes, I saw the hope of entire generations. They awaited the arrival of a redeemer, and I, although they didn't yet know it, was that redeemer.

I approached the river with determination. I knew I must submit to John's baptism, even though there was no sin in my heart to purify. John himself seemed hesitant when he saw me approaching. He knew the greatness of my arrival and when he saw me, he understood I was not worthy of being baptized. I responded with a calm look, knowing that I had to fulfill this act as the Bible states. "It is I who needs to be baptized by you," John said to me, his voice full of humility and reverence, " and you come to me?"

John didn't fully understand, but he accepted my request. With an obedience that came from the depths of my being, I immersed myself in the waters of the Jordan, and when I emerged, I felt something change within me. It wasn't just the water that surrounded me but the Holy Spirit descending upon me as a dove. It was a moment of purity, perfect communion with my Father, and His powerful and loving voice resounded in the heavens. "This is my beloved Son, in whom I am well pleased."

Baptism was the first visible act of my total obedience to my Father's will. It was as if, by immersing myself in the waters of the Jordan, I was utterly surrendering myself to the mission that awaited me. I realized it was more than a symbol. It was a step to keep promises made to Israel. It was almost time to fulfill what had been prophesied years ago.

When I emerged from the water, heaven seemed to bear witness. My Father's voice was clear and loud and, although those present did not fully understand, I knew it was confirmation that the time had come. It was the beginning of my public ministry and the manifestation that my relationship with the Father was perfectly aligned. My mission was more significant than anything people could understand. My Father chose me and the intention behind that choice was for the entire world.

What happened next was unlike anything I had ever felt before. As I rose from the waters, the heavens seemed to open and the Spirit of God came upon me, gentle like a dove but powerful beyond words. At that moment, something deep within me awakened completely—the calling I had carried in silence for so long now burned with clarity. I knew then—I was the Lamb, chosen to carry the weight of the world's sin. My Father had confirmed it. His voice echoed not just around me but through me. There was no more doubt, no more waiting. My Father had marked the path and I had to follow it regardless of the cost.

After this baptism, I didn't stay long with the crowd there. The Spirit led me to the desert, a lonely place of trial. My Father's voice continued to echo within me, guiding me toward what I must face. I was there for forty days, without eating or drinking, meditating on the mission that awaited me. In the desert, I prepared for the challenges that would come, for the trials and temptations that Satan would try to place in my path. I needed to go through that time of solitude, inner searching, and total alignment with God's will.

In the following days, I found myself alone, hungry, and weak in the wilderness. That's where the enemy came. He didn't come with force but with whispers. He tempted me with comfort, power, and glory. He showed me kingdoms and offered me their thrones if only I would bow to him. But I knew who I belonged to. My Father's voice was louder than any lie. I stood firm, not because it was easy but because I knew my purpose was more significant than anything this world could offer. Obedience to my Father meant everything to me—it still does.

My baptism wasn't just a sign of surrender—it marked the beginning of something holy. From that moment on, the Spirit didn't leave me. He walked with me, gave me strength when I felt empty and direction when the road ahead was unclear. My quiet life in Nazareth was behind me. The time of waiting was over. The world was about to see the light that had remained hidden for so long. I didn't seek attention but couldn't hide from the call. My Father had spoken and the time had come. And I was ready.

One night, as I meditated in the desert, I realized I had received an anointing to heal the sick, give hope to the lost, and set the captives free. My heart burned with a deep love for the people of Israel and the whole world. I knew the road would be difficult, that the religious and political authorities would reject me, and that my life would end on the cross. But that thought didn't frighten me. My Father's will was more important than everything else.

Leaving the desert, I returned to Galilee to begin my public ministry. I had been baptized, anointed by the Spirit, and called to fulfill a mission of redemption for all. People would see in me what so many had hoped for: the promised Messiah, the Son of God, the world's Savior. But there was still much to do and I was ready to fulfill everything entrusted to me by my Father.

My return to Galilee began a new chapter in my life. People in my area had heard of me, but many still saw me as the carpenter's son, a simple man from Nazareth. However, something had changed. The power of the Holy Spirit had manifested within me and I could no longer delay my mission. I knew I would go to the villages and towns, preaching the Gospel of the Kingdom of God and healing the sick, as foretold by the prophets.

I first headed to the synagogue in Nazareth, my hometown, where everyone had known me since childhood. When I arrived there, I was offered a reading from the Scriptures, as was customary for men in the community. I took the scroll of Isaiah and read the passage that spoke of the Spirit of the Lord being upon me and how I was sent by my Father to bring good news to the poor and also to proclaim liberty to the captives; to recover sight for the blind and set all the oppressed free. When I finished reading, I closed the scroll and looked at those present. I proclaimed in a firm and determined voice, "Today, I have fulfilled my Father's promise to you."

A murmur ran through the room. Some were surprised, but others felt uncomfortable because they knew what I said implied something profound. They saw me as an average man, the son of Joseph. They couldn't see that the young man they grew up with was now claiming to be the fulfillment of the prophecies.

Many were confused. Some even doubted me, wondering how such an ordinary man could be the fulfillment of what Isaiah had foretold. Rejection set in but, although the men of Nazareth couldn't see beyond my humanity, I knew that my identity didn't depend on what they thought of me. My true identity came from God, my Father, who had anointed my life to be a light to the nations.

Not everyone welcomed me when I first began to speak. The crowds came, yes—they were hungry for hope, for healing—but many didn't understand what I truly came to offer. The religious leaders especially looked at me with suspicion, even contempt. They clung to their traditions, their laws, their status. They couldn't see that the heart of God was never about rigid rules—it was about mercy, justice, and love. A love that reaches into the mess and lifts the broken. Still, I kept going. I couldn't stop, not with so many souls lost and suffering. I walked from village to village, speaking of a Kingdom built on grace, not power or pride. I invited sinners—yes, the outcasts, the forgotten, the ones deemed unworthy. I challenged the ones who thought they had it all figured out. I said clearly, "You can follow all the laws but still miss God's heart. If your heart lacks humility and love, you cannot establish a true connection with Him."

The miracles stirred people up even more. I saw the blind open their eyes for the first time. I touched the untouchable—the lepers—and their skin became clean. I wept with grieving families and then called their loved ones back from death. But even then, I told them, "Don't look at me as if I'm some spectacle. What you see—it's the Father working through me."

At first, there were few disciples, but as my message spread, more people began to follow me. I chose twelve men: simple fishermen, a tax collector, and a few others who had little in common with one another but who were called by me to be my witnesses and partners in the work I was about to accomplish. I taught them to love their neighbors, to forgive their enemies, and to live according to the principles of the Kingdom of God.

One of the most significant moments was when Peter, one of my closest disciples, proclaimed that I was the Christ, the Son of God. At that moment, I understood that my mission was to preach and form a community of believers who would take my message to the world. I taught them that, although the road would be difficult, God's love would always be with them.

People followed me for different reasons. Some did so for the miracles, others out of curiosity. Still, I wanted everyone to experience the Father's love and understand that the Kingdom of God was not a kingdom of worldly power but peace, justice, and reconciliation. I wanted everyone to experience what it meant to be truly free: free from sin, condemnation, and the world's lies.

I felt my heart fill with compassion for the multitudes. I saw the suffering of the sick, the marginalized, and those oppressed by Rome. I realized my mission was both spiritual and practical. I saw lives change while I healed the sick, freed captives and preached the Gospel. But I also understood that my time on Earth would not be eternal.

I always knew my purpose was deeper than healing broken bodies or teaching lessons in the synagogue. I came to show the world the heart of my Father, to speak of a love that never gives up—one that forgives, restores, and makes all things new. That's what I came to proclaim: the way back to God for everyone.

My heart broke for them. I saw it all—the sick left alone in their pain, the ones society pushed aside like they didn't matter, the weary souls crushed beneath the weight of Roman rule and daily survival. They weren't just faces in a crowd to me. I felt their sorrow deep in my spirit. Their pain became mine.

I didn't come just to preach sermons or perform miracles— that was only part of it. I came to step into their suffering, to walk with them in the darkness, to show them that God had not forgotten them. There was something bigger at work— something eternal—a love that could lift the heaviest burden, a hope that could breathe life into the most shattered heart.

I knew that my mission would culminate in my sacrifice on the cross, at which point humanity would find proper redemption. But before that, my life was to be a constant teaching, an example of living under God's will and loving God and my neighbor.

Thus, my ministry continued, always with an eye toward the divine purpose that had begun with my baptism in the Jordan

River. Every word, miracle, and act of mercy brought me closer to fulfilling what my Father had called me to do. It was not just about healing the sick or teaching eternal truths but about preparing for salvation through my sacrifice on the cross.

CHAPTER 5

PREACHING AND MIRACLES

— ·· •◦• ·· —

My ministry expanded beyond the borders of my homeland, Galilee. My message about the Kingdom of God became clear after my baptism in the Jordan River and the trials in the desert. Those days grew longer and the crowds grew more prominent. People came from all over, seeking healing, comfort, or simply a word of hope. I saw a mixture of suffering, despair, and longing in their eyes. My duty was to give them what they needed: the truth and life.

I clearly remember the first great sermon I gave, the famous Sermon on the Mount. A large crowd from different regions surrounded me. Some were looking for signs, others came to see what the talk was about, and some wanted to hear what I had to say. When they heard me talking, they were captivated by my words. They soon understood that my words offered more than their eyes could perceive. My message was not one of earthly power or political conquest; my message was about internal transformation, the regeneration of the heart.

I told them about the blessings of the Kingdom—how the poor in spirit, the grieving, the gentle, and those desperate for righteousness were the ones closest to God's heart. I could see it in their eyes—they were listening as if their souls had been waiting their whole lives to hear those words.

People listened attentively. Often, people thought the Kingdom of God was for the powerful, rich, and wise, but I taught them that it was for the humble, those who recognized their need for God. The crowds listened attentively, but there was deep confusion among them. How could it be that the poor and the weak were blessed? This message of the reversal of values shook their hearts. I wasn't there to give people more rules to follow or to help make them look holy on the outside. That was never the point. The Kingdom I spoke about goes deeper. It's about the heart, about real change; not just doing good but being renewed from the inside out. That's where God meets us—in transforming who we are, not how perfect we can pretend to be.

My message was clear: the Kingdom of God was not based on outward appearances or on the observance of superficial rules but on a profound transformation of the human being. God's true justice was not the justice of men but justice from a pure heart that loved God and neighbor.

"Do not think that I have come to abolish the Law or the Prophets," I told them, "but to fulfill them." My mission was not to destroy what God had established but to show the proper path to the complete restoration of humanity.

I tried to make it simple for them. What I came to say wasn't about looking religious or following every rule to be seen by others. That's not what the Kingdom of God is about. It's about something much deeper. It's about being changed from the inside out—your heart, mind, and whole life.

God's justice isn't like the justice people are used to. It's not about handing out punishments or pointing fingers. It's about a pure heart, a heart that loves—loves God and loves people. That's the kind of justice that matters in the Kingdom.

As my message spread, crowds kept coming, eager to hear, understand, and see more miracles. My fame spread throughout the region of Galilee and people brought me their sick, blind, and paralyzed. Seeing how many people were suffering surprised me. Still, it was uplifting to witness God's mercy working through me. I healed the sick, cast out demons, and raised the dead. Each miracle showed that the Kingdom of God had come.

I remember once, in the city of Capernaum, a person with paralysis was brought to me by his friends. Seeing the faith of those who brought the man to me, I said to them, "God forgives your sins." The Pharisees and the law teachers were outraged when they heard me say this. They thought that only God could forgive sins and, in their minds, I was committing blasphemy. But to show them that the Son of Man can forgive sins, I told the paralytic, "Get up, take up your mat, and go home." And so he did, just like that. The crowd was stunned—silent at first then amazed. But that moment wasn't just about showing power. It was about showing them something more profound: that the authority I carried came from my Father in heaven—and that real healing, absolute freedom, begins with faith.

Every miracle I performed wasn't just an act of mercy, though mercy was always at the center. It was a sign, a glimpse of what the Kingdom of God looks like. When I touched the sick and made them whole, I wasn't just healing their bodies—I was giving them back their dignity, reminding them that they were seen and loved by God.

And when I called the dead back to life, it wasn't just to shock people—it was to show them that death doesn't get the final word in my Father's Kingdom. Life does. That's why I came—to bring that life to everyone who would receive it.

But the truth is it was never just about physical healing. I wanted the crowd to see past the pain in their bodies and recognize the need in their souls. They needed a new heart, life, and fresh beginning that could only come from God. And that's what I came to offer.

There was something about it that not only healed people physically but also touched them spiritually. I saw many who, upon being healed, became my followers, but I also saw those who, despite being healed, turned away, unable to understand the depth of my message. The Kingdom of God was not only for those seeking a temporary solution to their problems but for those willing to surrender their lives to God's will, to live under the reign of His love and justice.

The teaching about the Kingdom of God became the central focus of everything I did. It wasn't a philosophy or a moral lesson. It was the start of a new reality among them. This reality would change every part of human life. I showed them that the Kingdom of God isn't a distant future. It's already present among them through my words and miracles. And yet, for many, the Kingdom was not something they could see with their eyes because it was a Kingdom seen and understood only through the eyes of the heart.

At the end of each day, when I was alone with my disciples, I spoke to them more deeply about the Kingdom of God, the cross that awaited me, and how they should follow in my footsteps. I taught them to be humble, serve others, and not seek greatness or recognition. I knew I was showing them a path of sacrifice, suffering, and eternal life. I asked them to take up their crosses and follow me because the Kingdom of God is built not with power but with love, not with riches but with generosity, not with oppression but with forgiveness.

And so, each day, my mission deepened as I preached and healed. The miracles continued and the crowds grew, but I truly desired each person to find the peace and freedom that only my Father can give. That was my greatest miracle: to lead every human being into a personal relationship with the Father, a relationship that would transform not only their bodies but their hearts.

My ministry continued to grow. At first, many thought the Kingdom of God was a physical place, something they could see with their eyes, but little by little, they understood that it was not an earthly kingdom but a spiritual reality that invaded people's hearts and lives. I taught them that the Kingdom of God is within them. It's not a place far away. It's something they experience through a real relationship with the Father.

Not everyone reacted the same way when I spoke. Some people were joyful, feeling seen, heard, and finally understood. They praised God because the words I spoke gave them hope. But others grew angry—especially those in power. My message was a relief to the lowly and those struggling in life. But to those holding on to power and status, it seemed like a threat.

The religious leaders struggled the most. I wasn't trying to provoke them, but the truth I spoke cut through the surface of their system. It challenged the very structure they built their lives on. And that made them uncomfortable; afraid, even. They saw me as dangerous because I wasn't playing by their rules.

But I couldn't allow their rejection to stop me. Their disapproval didn't change what I knew deep in my soul—my mission came from the Father. I wasn't here to win approval or to fit in. I came to bring the truth, even if that truth stirred things up. We should have been ready to receive it.

There were times when crowds would gather to listen to me for hours. On one occasion, when I was preaching about God's love and mercy, and seeing that the day was drawing late, I knew people were hungry. They were listening to me preach for hours. I asked my disciples if we had any food and they told me there was not enough.

I still remember the looks on their faces—thousands of hungry and tired people sitting on that hillside. All we had were five loaves of bread and two fish. It didn't seem like enough, not even close. But I took what they gave me, lifted it to heaven, and talked to my Father. Immediately, the bread and fish multiplied. Then we started passing it out. Everyone was amazed. The disciples passed basket after basket until every single person had enough. And after everybody ate more than once, we still had leftovers.

That moment wasn't just about food—it was about trust. It was about what can happen when we bring what little we have and place it in the hands of the Father. I wanted them to see that faith opens the door to provision. Even when it looks like we don't have enough, God can take what's small and make it more than enough—for everyone.

My miracles were not just about physical healing or material provision. Each miracle illustrated how God works in the invisible men's example; when I healed a man born blind, the people were amazed. It wasn't just about restoring sight to the blind but about showing that the genuinely blind person was the hardened heart of those who believed themselves to be righteous without mercy. That miracle also reminded them of their spiritual darkness and how only the Son could give them the light of truth.

My calling also included teaching everyone to live according to Kingdom values. I taught them that they should not seek recognition or glory and that the truly great person in God's Kingdom is the one who becomes a servant of others. Once upon a time, the disciples argued about who would be the greatest. I told them something surprising: "To be first, you must be willing to be last. If you want to become great, then serve—serve everyone."

It wasn't a clever saying. I meant it. In my Kingdom, greatness isn't about being important or admired. It's not about titles or being in control. You find true greatness in humility—in bending down to lift someone else up. I wanted them to understand that real leadership is love in action. It means washing feet, not standing on a pedestal. It means choosing the low place, even when you could demand the highest. That's the kind of life I came to live—and the kind of heart I hoped they'd choose to follow.

I taught them by example, serving others, touching lepers, healing the sick, and speaking to those despised by society, such as tax collectors and women of ill repute. My life was an invitation to break down the barriers that separate people, to look beyond social differences, and to see every human being as a creation loved by God.

One of the most challenging teachings I gave was when I spoke about the need to take up our cross. I knew this message would be challenging to understand because they did not think of suffering as something positive. However, I shared that anyone who wants to save their life will lose it. But if you lose your life for me, you will find it instead. "The Kingdom of God is not about worldly power and victory but sacrifice and surrender." I spoke to them about denying ourselves and putting God and others above our desires and ambitions. This message was a challenge for many, but it was the foundation of the Christian life.

Walking from town to town, I also shared parables, profound yet down-to-earth stories that revealed the truth of the Kingdom of God. I told them about the sower who sowed seeds in different types of soil, the lost sheep, the Good Samaritan, and the mustard seed that, although small, grew into a large tree. Each parable aimed to open hearts so people could see the spiritual truth behind the physical. I showed them that the Kingdom of God spread humbly and silently but that, over time, it would produce abundant fruit. Each would have a divine purpose, and I desired all who heard me to open their hearts and receive the Word with faith.

I didn't hold back regarding pride and hypocrisy; I had to speak the truth. I saw too many who wore holiness like a mask. People looked righteous on the outside, said all the right things, and followed every ritual, but inside, their hearts were far from God. That disheartened me because the

Kingdom isn't about looking good—it's about being good. It's about a clean heart, not just hands that appear clean.

I tried to show them the power of humility, of knowing that we're all fragile and in need. I told them, "Don't think of yourself as being better than anyone else. Don't walk around pretending you have it all together." The Father isn't looking for perfect people; He's looking for honest hearts—people who know their need for Him and live in love, not judgment.

I knew the pathway I was calling them toward wouldn't be easy. The way to the Kingdom is narrow. Not many are willing to walk it because it requires surrender, humility and trust. But I always held on to hope—that maybe, just maybe, hearts would open. They would listen, really listen, and find the life created for them, a life shaped by love, truth, and a deep, daily walk with God.

I also warned them about the dangers of pride and hypocrisy. I saw many religious leaders. They claimed to be righteous on the outside, but inside, evil filled them. I told them that God's Kingdom was not measured by appearances but by a pure heart and life's sincerity. I spoke to them about the importance of humility, recognizing our limitations and dependencies, and never believing ourselves superior to others. I knew the path to the Kingdom was narrow and that few would find it. I hoped everyone would hear and follow the path of truth. We see this truth through a deep relationship with God. It's lived out in love, humility, and obedience.

Miracles kept happening and many people believed in me. But some, like the religious leaders, did not. At times, their questions were tricky and aimed to challenge me. Still, I always responded with insight and clarity. They recognized my words were wise, but they couldn't accept them. They felt challenged by their own beliefs. They knew I didn't like them and didn't follow their rules. I never stopped loving them, even after their rejection. It hurt to see their lack of faith. Sometimes, I told them I didn't judge them but came so that all might have life. I loved them, but I knew their cold hearts stopped them from seeing what was ahead.

My ministry included teachings, miracles, and signs; yet, my main goal was to prepare people for what lay ahead. I knew my time on Earth wouldn't last forever. Every day brought me closer to the ultimate sacrifice I was to make for humanity. Even with the challenges, my heart stayed true to the mission the Father gave me. Every step I took, every miracle I performed brought me closer to the cross. But my hope was never only for this world. I knew my sacrifice would bring eternal life to all who believed in me.

The Miracles

Throughout my ministry, I performed many miracles, showing God's presence and divine power among men. But they weren't just displays of power. Every healing, every wonder came from a place of deep compassion. I wasn't trying to impress the crowds; I wanted them to see the Father—His mercy, closeness, and love for the broken and overlooked.

Those miracles were never just about wonders or signs. They were invitations—each one a doorway into something deeper, a glimpse of what the Kingdom of God truly looks like—a world made whole, where broken things are restored, where light overcomes the darkness and life flows freely again—just as the Father intended from the beginning.

And I still think about those moments. They happened a long time ago, but their meaning hasn't faded. If anything, they still speak—still stir faith, still bring hope. I want to tell you about them, not just so you'll know what I did but so you can understand why I did it and what it reveals about the heart of God.

I remember the moment I healed a man born blind. I was sitting near the entrance of a temple when someone asked me to have mercy on him. The man couldn't see because he was born blind. Taking some mud, I approached him, mixed it with saliva, and smeared it on his eyes. Then I told him, "Go home." The blind man obeyed without hesitation, and when he returned, he saw perfectly. The people couldn't believe what they were seeing. It wasn't only about giving them back their sight. It was also about revealing that true light comes from heaven. Only the Son can open their spiritual eyes.

On another occasion, I was at a friend's house and some men brought a paralytic to see me. The crowd was so large that they couldn't get close. They climbed onto the house's roof, made a hole, and lowered the man on his mat. I told the paralyzed man, "I have forgiven your sins." At that moment, the man got up, took his mat, and walked away.

The Pharisees and law teachers were furious. They thought only God could forgive sins. I wanted to show them that the Son of Man could forgive and heal. The people who were present were amazed and glorified God.

Another miracle I performed happened while crossing the Sea of Galilee. A great storm arose during the journey and the waves threatened to overturn our boat. The terrified disciples woke me, saying, "Lord, we are about to perish!" I got up, rebuked the wind and the water and, at that moment, everything calmed down. I asked them, "Why are you afraid, ye of little faith?" That miracle was a lesson about the peace that only God can give, even amid a storm. I calmed the sea and taught them that faith can bring peace, even when everything seems to be falling apart.

I also remember the moment I resurrected the daughter of Jairus, a synagogue leader. Jairus came to me in despair because his daughter was about to die. As we went to his house, we received the news that she had already passed away. The people were weeping, but I told them, "Do not weep, for she is not dead but asleep." When we arrived, I took her hand and said, "Talitha kumi," which means, "Little girl, I say to you, arise." At that moment, the girl rose and everyone was amazed. This miracle demonstrated that death isn't final in the Kingdom of God and that even the dead can return to life.

One day, I walked through the crowd with people pressing in from every side. I felt someone touch me while I was walking. It was not just a touch but something deeper inside me. Power had gone out of me. I stopped and asked, "Who touched me?" Not because I didn't know but because I wanted her to know she mattered. She came forward, shaking and afraid. This woman had suffered for years—bleeding constantly, cut off from her community, treated like she was unclean, untouchable. She had tried everything, seen every doctor, and spent all she had. But nothing worked. Until that moment—when she reached out, believing that just touching the edge of my cloak may be enough. I looked at her and said, "Your faith has healed you. Go in peace."

That miracle healed not only her body but also her soul. The weight of her shame was lifted. She regained her dignity. She was no longer invisible. She received care and love. That's the kind of healing I came to bring to the world so that humanity would know that only my Father has the power.

Every miracle I performed was an opportunity to teach about God's goodness and greatness. But my greatest desire was not only to heal bodies but also to heal hearts. True transformation happens when people see the need for change inside themselves. This change can only come from God's love. Every miracle invites us to trust God, walk in faith, and experience His Kingdom, which is close and among us.

CHAPTER 6

CONFLICTS AND OPPOSITION

———— ··●·· ————

My time on Earth wasn't easy. From the beginning, I walked into a world that was suffering and lost. So many hearts were closed off—people had turned to empty idols, lifeless statues, chasing after gods that couldn't hear, couldn't speak, couldn't love. They were searching but didn't know what they were looking for.

And when I came with the truth—with the message of a living God, the One who formed them, loved them, and longed to restore them—I was rejected. Not once or twice, but again and again. Some laughed. Some walked away. Others got angry—especially those whose power and pride were threatened by what I said.

I felt their rejection. I carried the weight of it. But I never gave up because I knew who sent me. I knew my Father's heart and that kept me going. I came to show them that God is not far off or silent but present, alive and full of mercy. My mission was to wake people up, to call them back to the truth: that they were created in love, for love, by a God who awaits them with open arms; to break down thoughts and beliefs that kept humanity from God's purpose. As my ministry grew, the opposition also increased. Many felt my message threatened their authority, power, and traditions.

The religious leaders, the Pharisees, Sadducees, and scribes, began to see me as a threat. At first, they were curious about my teachings. But they soon realized that my words challenged their laws and beliefs. They also learned the hypocrisy surrounding them. I clearly remember the first confrontation I had with them. One day, while teaching in a synagogue, a man came to me with a withered hand, asking for healing on the Sabbath. The Pharisees and scribes observed intently, waiting to see whether I would break the law. They knew that the Sabbath law forbids doing work and, in their minds, healing was work. However, seeing their hardness of heart, I asked them, "Do you think it is lawful to do good on the Sabbath? To save a life or to kill?" They didn't answer and, at that moment, I healed the man's hand. I wanted to show them that the Sabbath isn't about oppression. I wanted to show them that the law aimed to give life, not death. But they didn't want to understand. They became enraged and began to plan how to destroy me.

The evil I saw in those religious leaders was heartbreaking. I wondered how they could be so ruthless. They spoke of purity and justice, but their hearts were proud and selfish. They turned the law into a tool to highlight their power. They sought recognition and control, prioritizing them over mercy or justice. I often told them, "You scribes and Pharisees are hypocrites! You block entry into the Kingdom of Heaven. You yourselves cannot enter and you also block entry for others." I criticized them for interpreting the law because they used it to cling to their power and status, oppressing the people in the process.

My teachings about love, mercy, and humility challenged their beliefs. For them, strict rules and perfect observance of the law formed the basis of God's justice. I showed them true justice comes from a sincere heart and love for God and neighbor. I explained that it wasn't what they ate that made them unclean. It was what came out of their mouths, challenging their beliefs about purity.

But it wasn't the only Pharisees and scribes who opposed me. Also, the Sadducees, who were religious leaders, were linked to political power and the temple. These men didn't believe in the resurrection of the dead, angels, or the Spirit. When I talked to them about life after death, they challenged me. I explained that those who sacrifice for God's Kingdom will gain eternal life. They tried to trap me with a riddle. It was about a woman with several husbands. They asked, "In the resurrection, which of the seven will she be the wife of?" My answer was clear: I told them that no one will marry when the time of resurrection comes. They will live like angels in heaven, in an atmosphere of peace and happiness forever. Hearing this, they remained silent. My answer showed the truth about eternal life and challenged their way of viewing the faith.

Once, someone asked me about the greatest commandment of the law. They were expecting a conflicting answer. But I told them, "You must love the Lord your God with all your heart, soul, and mind. You must love your neighbor as yourself." These words contained no contradiction, only the truth that fulfilled the law. The Pharisees and Sadducees focused on external laws. They didn't realize that love was the proper foundation of justice and piety.

My constant clashes with religious leaders led us to a deeper conflict. I experienced a continuous struggle between the old and new teachings. I tried to teach them about love, humility, and forgiveness, but they wouldn't admit it; they felt threatened by my teachings. They saw me as their enemy. They knew that, through my teachings, they could lose control of their people. My teachings challenged their understanding of the law they had taught for years.

They tried to discredit me and trap me with their questions. I remember them asking me if it was lawful to pay taxes to Caesar, trying to turn me against Roman power. But I replied, "Give to Caesar the things that are Caesar's and to God the things that are God's." My answer left them speechless. I wasn't against the Roman authorities, but I was teaching them that their greatest loyalty was to God, not earthly powers.

Opposition came not only from religious leaders but also from the people themselves. Many felt uncomfortable with my teachings; they challenged their expectations of a warrior Messiah who would free them from the Roman yoke. My message of love and peace was not what they expected and some began to abandon me. Many of my disciples were disconcerted and I asked them, "Do you also want to leave?"

To which Peter replied, "Lord, to whom shall we go? You have the words of eternal life."

My life on this earth was tough. Every step I took felt like it brought me closer to conflict with those who opposed my message. I knew that not everyone would understand my mission and that many would turn away. However, I also learned that the Kingdom of God would spread, not by force but by the truth and light I brought. Opposition always gave me a chance to grow closer to the Father. Many may have rejected me, but I stayed true to God's plan.

The pressure from the religious leaders grew stronger. Each day, I sensed my journey was coming to an end. The Pharisees and Sadducees could no longer ignore me. Anger filled their hearts. There were times when they tried to arrest me, but they were unsuccessful because my time had not yet come. My mission rested in God's hands. He would choose the right time.

But as the opposition increased, I also saw many who believed in me and clung to the promises of the Kingdom of God. My message of love, forgiveness, and inner transformation did not fall in vain. I knew that, although the path was difficult, it would be worth it because the truth I brought would change their lives and the history of humanity itself. Although the religious leaders tried to stop me, they could not stop the power of God, which moved in every word, every miracle, and every teaching. Thus, my journey continued: a journey of conflict but also hope because, in opposition, I knew I was sowing seeds of eternal life, seeds that would grow and bear fruit long after my mission on this earth ended.

As conflicts with religious authorities increased, I found myself constantly challenged by those who wanted to discredit me. They tried to put me in a difficult position, to ensnare me with words and traps. On one occasion, I was asked about the greatest commandment of the law, hoping my answer would be contradictory. But I told them, "You shall love the Lord your God with all your heart, soul, and mind. You shall love your neighbor as yourself." These words contained no contradiction, only the truth that fulfilled the law. These Pharisees and Sadducees, meticulous about external laws, did not understand that love was the proper foundation of all justice and piety.

On another occasion, I spoke to them about the false prophets who would come, those who would dress in sheep's clothing but were wolves inside. My words were to those who used faith for their benefit, manipulating the weakest and exploiting the people's devotion. They knew my criticism was a mirror reflecting their sins, which hurt them, so more and more of them looked for ways to trap me, wanting me to contradict myself or make a mistake.

But, despite all this, I never lost hope. My mission was not to impose myself but to guide people toward the truth and light of God. I knew some truly listened, desired to change, and understood the Kingdom's message. My task was to sow the seed and, even though many strayed, I trusted that, in time, the seed would grow in sincere hearts; those souls who would not allow themselves to be trapped by empty traditions and the selfishness of religious leaders.

CHAPTER 7

THE LAST SUPPER
AND THE BETRAYAL

———— · · ●· · ————

Passover, the most important festival for the people of Israel, was approaching, and I felt in my heart that the time of my mission on Earth was about to end. I knew that my sacrifice was inevitable, that the events that would happen in those days would forever change the course of human history. Therefore, that day, as I gathered my disciples for the Last Supper, everything was imbued with profound gravity.

The meal began in an atmosphere of solemnity, although my disciples could not yet grasp the magnitude of what was about to happen. They thought we were celebrating just another Passover, like so many others, but I knew this would be the last time I would be with them in that way. I felt deeply close to them, like a teacher preparing to depart, but also like a friend who deeply loves his followers.

The moment arrived when I took the bread, blessed it, broke it, and gave it to my disciples. I told them to eat it and that the bread was my body, which was given to them. I took the cup of wine and, after giving thanks, I also gave it to my disciples and told them it was my blood, which was shed for them. In this way, I instituted the Eucharist, a sacrament that would be the eternal bond between God and humanity, a sign of my sacrifice and immense love for all. The bread was my body and the wine was my blood. I would shed my blood to forgive sins.

At that moment, a heavy mood fell over the table, as if everyone sensed something was wrong. I knew that among the twelve disciples, one of them would betray me. My soul was troubled, but I had to fulfill what the Father had arranged. I told them, "Assuredly, I say to you, one of you will betray me."

My disciples looked at one another, confused and dismayed. Peter, who was standing nearby, asked me, "Is it I, Lord?" And all the others did the same.

I answered them, "Whoever dips the bread with me is the one who will betray me." While I was speaking, Judas Iscariot, who had already made the pact with the chief priests to betray me, dipped the bread in the sauce and gave it to me. I told him, "What you must do, do it quickly." The others didn't understand then, but Judas, sensing their hardened hearts, left the dinner to fulfill his sad destiny.

The atmosphere was charged with sadness but also with love. I knew the disciples would abandon me and the trial would be great for all, but my heart was still full of compassion for them. After Judas left, I spoke to them about the importance of loving one another as a sign that they would be my faithful followers. I told them, "A new commandment I give you: Love one another. As I have loved you, you also should love one another." In my anguish, I continued instructing them about what should happen and how to live after my departure.

When dinner was over, we headed to the Mount of Olives. Upon arriving at the Garden of Gethsemane, I felt a great anguish in my soul. The weight of the world's sin and the suffering I was about to endure invaded me with an unbearable intensity. I knew my sacrifice was near when one of my disciples was going to deliver me to the sinners. Deep trouble filled my soul. While some of my disciples were resting, I took Peter, James, and John with me to pray

At that moment, I spoke to the Father. My soul was anguished; the weight of the mission was too great, but I submitted to God's will. Then we returned to my disciples and found them asleep. I asked them why they could not watch with me for one hour. I separated from them and prayed again. I felt my heart break and I experienced a moment of loneliness. Even though my disciples were around me, I had to face the sacrifice alone. I couldn't rely on the world at that moment.

After finishing my prayer, I returned to the disciples and asked them to rise and let us behold. I said that the man who betrayed me was at hand. At that moment, I saw Judas approaching, accompanied by a group of soldiers with torches and swords. Judas saw us, approached me, and kissed me—the sign with which he would hand me over to my enemies. I asked him, "Do you betray the Son of God with a kiss?" He didn't respond, but his betrayal was complete; there was nothing to do then.

Seeing what was happening, the disciples were terrified and asked me if they should defend me. Peter, impulsive as ever, drew his sword and cut off the ear of one of the high priest's servants. Immediately, I ordered him to put the sword back in its scabbard. At that moment, I healed the man's ear, showing them that my path was not one of violence but of peace and forgiveness.

I was arrested and taken before the Sanhedrin, the council of religious leaders, where they falsely accused me of blasphemy. They could find no witnesses who would truthfully accuse me, but in the end, they asked me if I was the Christ, the Son of the Blessed One, and I replied, "Yes, I am." These words were enough to condemn me to death because they recognized in them a claim to divinity. They spat on me, hit me, and humiliated me, but I remained silent, doing the Father's will.

At dawn, they took me before Pontius Pilate, the Roman governor. Pilate found no fault in me. He knew they gave me up because of envy. The crowd, led by the religious leaders, shouted, "Crucify him! Crucify him!" I felt the heavy burden of rejection from all the people who had welcomed me with hosannas just a few days before.

Fearful of a revolt, Pilate washed his hands and told the crowd that he was innocent of the blood of me, a righteous man. "It's up to you." Then they handed me over to be flogged.

They stripped me of my clothes and dressed me in a purple robe. I felt the weight of mockery and contempt for my human dignity. They placed a crown of thorns on me, and while the soldiers mocked me, saying to me, "Hail, King of the Jews," I didn't respond. I knew this was part of the suffering I had to endure. Finally, I had to carry my cross to Mount Calvary, where it would all end.

I can't compare the agony of the betrayal at Gethsemane to anything. But the agony of Gethsemane was nothing compared to what was to come. I knew they would crucify me; there was no turning back. I had come into the world to give my life and every step I took brought me closer to fulfilling God's will. The cross awaited, but I knew that, through my death, humanity could find salvation. My mission remained clear: I must surrender and do my Father's will.

As I walked toward Calvary, I fell several times from the weight of the cross. But I couldn't give up. My love for humanity drove me and motivated me. I knew my suffering would open the gates of heaven for everyone.

CHAPTER 8

PASSION, DEATH, AND RESURRECTION

The weight of the cross was unbearable. My heart pounded with the painful certainty of what must happen. The moment had come; the Passion had begun and the world's salvation depended on my sacrifice. The soldiers guarding me laughed while some struck me. The crowd surrounded me, shouting and cheering. Some cursed me while others cried in silence. I saw familiar faces, ones who followed me and loved me. I watched their hope fade away. I saw my mother, Mary, in the crowd. Her eyes reflected indescribable suffering. Her heart was also being pierced by a sword, as Simeon had said years before.

I fell under the weight of the cross. But Simon, a man from Cyrene, helped me carry it. He was not one of my followers, but his presence at that moment was a reminder that, even in adversity, the help of others can be a sign of God's mercy. I couldn't help but think that, at that moment, my burden was that of all the men and women who had come and would come.

When I reached Mount Calvary, they stripped me of my clothes, leaving me exposed to the world. They nailed my hands and feet to the cross and, although the physical pain was indescribable, what tore me apart most was the feeling of abandonment. He who had never known sin and had always been in perfect communion with the Father now felt separated from Him. In that moment, hanging there, the pain was beyond anything I could describe. Every breath felt like fire in my lungs and my heart was heavy. Not only did I feel pain in my body, but I also carried the weight of the world's brokenness and sin that I chose to take on.

My crucifixion was a scene of pain and suffering but also of immense love. The crowd mocked me and dishonored me, challenging me to save myself if I indeed were the Son of God. The chief priests, Pharisees, and scribes came to me. They said, "He saved others; yet he cannot save himself."

And then it just burst out of me, the words, "My God, my God, why have You left Me?" It wasn't doubt but the cry of a Son in the middle of total darkness, feeling the full cost of surrender.

I still held on to the Father's purpose, even though I couldn't feel His presence. The cross wasn't just torture. It was love— in its rawest, most painful form. I gave everything there— blood, breath, my very life. And even in that horror, something holy was unfolding—a rescue, a redemption, for every single person.

One of the criminals crucified at my side insulted me. The other man saw the wrong in our punishment. He looked at me and said, "Jesus, remember me in your Kingdom."

I replied, "Today, you will be with me in paradise." At that moment, compassion filled my heart. I was grateful because, even though many rejected me, some understood God's mercy even during their last hour.

My mother, Mary, was standing next to John, the beloved disciple. I looked at my mother, my heart overflowing with love and compassion. I knew she was suffering. Her tears ran over her face and she looked at me with sadness. She felt my pain.

Then I spoke to her: "Woman, behold your son." And to John I said, "Behold your mother." In that act of love, I left my mother under the protection of John, my most faithful disciple. I kept thinking about how that painful moment turned into a deep act of love and care for those who came after me.

Finally, after hours of agony, I knew the end was near. I felt that God's love would take away my suffering, rejection, and humiliation. I surrendered my spirit to the Father. "Father, into your hands I commend my spirit." And with these words, I faced the end of my human life on the cross.

After my death, they took my body and placed it in a borrowed tomb belonging to Joseph of Arimathea. The disciples, fearful and filled with sadness, dispersed. They still didn't understand what had happened; they didn't understand that my death wasn't the end but the beginning of something much more significant. But in their hearts, they held the hope that the promise of the Kingdom would come true.

On the third day, while sadness filled the hearts of my followers, something extraordinary happened. The tomb where they had laid my body was empty. My body was no longer there. The stone at the tomb's entrance was rolled away and the news quickly spread among my disciples. Mary Magdalene was the first to see me resurrected. She was weeping by the tomb, looking for my body, but when she saw me, she didn't immediately recognize me. I asked her, "Why are you crying? Who are you looking for?" And when she spoke my name, I replied, "Mary." Her eyes opened and she recognized that I was alive. I told her, "Do not touch me, for I have not yet ascended to the Father. Go to my brothers and tell them that I am ascending to my Father and your Father; to my God and your God."

The resurrection was the confirmation that the Father had accepted my sacrifice. The victory over death, over sin, was complete. I appeared to my disciples on several occasions, showing them the wounds in my hands and my side so that they would believe it was truly me. To Thomas, who was doubting, I said, "Put your finger here and see my hands; put your hand in my side and do not be unbelieving, but believe."

I was with them for forty days, teaching them about the Kingdom of God and preparing their hearts for what would come next. I gave them a mission: "Go and make disciples of all nations, baptizing them in the name of the Father, the Son, and the Holy Spirit." And I promised them I would not leave them alone but send the Holy Spirit to guide them.

Before my final ascension to heaven, I gave them one last blessing: "I am with you always until the end of the age."

Then I looked at them and rose into heaven, leaving them hopeful for my return.

My Father's Son had defeated death. The resurrection had proven that God's love is stronger than death. My mission of redemption was complete, but my work in the hearts of humanity would continue. The resurrection was a victory for me and all who believe in me. Salvation had arrived and the Kingdom of God was open to all.

My resurrection was a testimony of divine power and a sign of hope for all who would believe in me. I had conquered death, but the true victory was the new beginning I had brought to humanity. My resurrection symbolized my victory over death—restoring the broken relationship between man and God. Anyone who believes in me and accepts my sacrifice for their sins will have eternal life.

My disciples, amazed and full of faith, started to realize what my resurrection meant. Each meeting with them showed us that the promise of the Kingdom of God was still alive. It felt closer than ever before. When I showed up, they saw me as a sign that the Kingdom of Heaven was manifesting on Earth.

As I met with them, I also instructed them about the mission that awaited them. I also told them they would never be alone even though I ascended to heaven. The Holy Spirit would guide, strengthen, and empower them. They should share all my messages of salvation with everyone. I told them not to be afraid. God's love would spread everywhere, changing hearts and lives. I rose to heaven, but I'm still with everyone who follows me now and forever.

At first, my disciples felt scared and confused. Then the Holy Spirit empowered them. They started to preach the Gospel with courage and strong resolve. They were the first to see the new life in me. Their testimony, along with mine, laid the foundation for the church, which would grow for centuries. I ascended to heaven and my disciples continued preaching everything I had taught them. My presence will continue with all who follow me today and always. Call on me if you need me and I will respond.

CHAPTER 9

MY LEGACY

• — • •●• • — •

As I ascended to heaven, I left behind a transformed earth and a message of love and salvation. I knew the road would be long; people still had a long way to go before they could understand my legacy. But I knew my disciples would spread the message I had left them throughout the world.

My ascension was the last visible act of my mission on Earth and, although I was no longer physically manifested, my spiritual presence remained with each of my followers, guiding them and strengthening their hearts.

My disciples were amazed by my resurrection. They watched as I ascended to heaven. They felt sadness, but their hearts were full of hope. They had seen the impossible: my death and resurrection. I entrusted them with a remarkable task, something they never imagined, to deliver my message of salvation to everyone.

When the angels appeared, they told them they would see me return as they had seen me leave. I knew they were afraid, but I also knew they could perform the mission I assigned to them.

The Holy Spirit would soon come and He would give them the strength and wisdom to carry my message beyond the borders of Israel, beyond anything they could have imagined. I taught them they had access to a direct relationship with the Father through me. I showed them how to live in love, humility, and compassion and left them examples of serving others and loving their neighbors as themselves. My mission was to give life, fix what's broken, heal human wounds, and guide others to salvation. In my departure, my message was to remain in their hearts and preach to every corner of the world.

Through my apostles, my teachings reached every corner of the Roman Empire and beyond. Those who walked beside me and saw me die and resurrect became the torchbearers of the faith. Despite persecutions, challenges, and trials, my message continued to spread. The followers who joined them formed communities of believers, small at first but which, over time, grew and spread throughout the entire world. In every corner of the empire, people proclaimed that the Kingdom of God was near, that salvation had arrived, and that whosoever believed in me would have everlasting life in the lap of the Father.

Christianity began to spread, not only through words but also through actions. Many of my followers embraced my teachings throughout their lives. They helped others, shared love without conditions, and discovered true peace. Each time my followers helped the sick, fed those in need or forgave others, they spread my message of love.

For centuries, my message of love and forgiveness ignited movements for justice, compassion, and renewal in societies. My life and sacrifice inspired people of all nations to seek peace, reconciliation, and justice. God's mercy embraced the poor and marginalized. Though imperfect and human, the Church became the body of believers called to live according to my teachings. I continue to share my message of hope through the Church and institutions that aim to show my love and service. They may have human errors, but they still strive to reflect the example and spirit of my mission.

Christianity transformed the world's culture and spirituality in ways my first disciples could not have imagined. Love of neighbor, forgiveness, solidarity, human dignity, and equality before God were values that my disciples and followers taught to societies on every continent. This message influenced religious institutions and political, economic, and cultural ones. My teachings inspired reform and human rights. They also sparked social justice and movements for human dignity.

When my followers looked back and saw all that had happened through the centuries, they understood that my sacrifice on the cross and my resurrection brought hope for the future and transformation for the present. Every heart that found faith, every life touched by my love, became a testimony of what God could do in the world through a single person willing to follow me. The miracles I performed during my time on Earth continued, in a different way, through the lives of those who followed me through my Holy Spirit.

Although my ascension marked my physical separation from my disciples, my presence lived on in them and every new believer. I was with them and will be with them through the Holy Spirit, the Comforter, who will guide the Church until the end. This promise was my final gift: you will never be alone. Although the trials will sometimes be great, the peace I left with you will be even greater. The mission I left to my disciples and all who believe in me will live forever. Every generation is responsible for carrying the torch of faith, sharing the Gospel of hope, and living as witnesses of the light that brings life to the world.

And even today, my legacy lives on. Every time someone prays, forgives, or serves with love, my Spirit continues to work in the world. At its core, Christianity is not a religion of rules but a call to a transformative relationship with the Creator. This relationship began with my life, death, and resurrection and continues through the centuries.

Reflecting on history, I rejoice when I see the profound impact of what I began in my final years on Earth. It was not a religious movement but a transformation for humanity. After more than 2,000 years, I know many keep following me. Although I know others have strayed from me, I do not lose hope that they will understand that I am the truth and the life. Every act of love, service, and forgiveness is an act of my presence, of my life in each of you. Through my sacrifice, God's eternal love has touched the world and that love continues to touch hearts, heal wounds, and transform lives.

My legacy lives on through my followers and in the hearts changed by God's love. Those who believed in me received an abstract faith and an invitation to live a new reality. This new reality is not just a hope for the future but a manifestation of the Kingdom of God in the present. Every restored life and healed heart shows that the Kingdom of Heaven is here. It may not be fully complete yet, but its presence is clear.

My legacy is more than words or teachings. It is an invitation to live God's love, share it with others, and be instruments of peace and reconciliation in a divided world. Just as the Holy Spirit came to guide my first disciples, today he continues to guide those who dare to follow me, to take up my cross, and to live in the power of my resurrection.

My disciples traveled, preached, and built communities. They shared my words and the love I showed them. My message has faced distortion over time, but its essence remains. It thrives in those who have taken my cross and followed my path. Every sacrifice of love, act of kindness, and justice reflects my Spirit at work throughout the world.

What began in a small corner of the world in a forgotten village expanded through the centuries and reached the earth's most remote corners. My teachings on mercy, forgiveness and human dignity have influenced movements that have fought for justice, equality, and peace. The Church, though imperfect, has been the vehicle through which the message of salvation has arrived, not only through its words but also through its actions.

Every generation of Christians is responsible for transmitting this light, living according to the principles of love and sacrifice that I established for them. Today, in every corner of the world, my Spirit guides those who follow me, reminding them that my love knows no bounds, that my sacrifice was for all, and that the mission of expanding the

Kingdom of God remains a constant calling. The message of love, hope, and redemption continues to expand. And this is my promise: I will be with you until the end of the age.

CHAPTER 10

PARABLES

When I preached in different places, I shared simple stories with the crowds so they could understand my message. These stories touched the hearts and opened the minds of those who heard them. I called these stories "parables." They revealed profound truths and challenged common beliefs about the Kingdom of God. I told them stories through simple images and situations so they would understand me. Anyone could understand them. They had profound meanings that contained a moral and religious education, revealing a spiritual truth comparatively.

I didn't speak with grand philosophical discourses or complicated theories but with images and situations that anyone could understand, but they had a much deeper meaning.

The Parable of the Sower

One of the most well-known stories I told was that of a sower who went out to sow his seeds. He scattered them. Some fell from his hands and birds ate them. Others landed on rocky ground, so they dried up without deep roots. Some fell among thorns that choked them. But some fell on good soil, where they produced a plentiful harvest.

This simple parable speaks of how the Word of God falls on human hearts. Some reject it, others receive it only for a time, and others allow the world's cares to drown it. But those who receive it with a willing and open heart will bear abundant fruit. Each of you can receive that seed in your heart, but whether the soil is ready to accept it and allow it to grow depends on you.

The Parable of the Good Samaritan

Two important people, a priest and a Levite ignored a man who lay wounded and abandoned by the side of the road. But a Samaritan, considered by many to be an enemy, stopped, cared for him, and paid attention to him. When I told this parable, I taught them that genuine compassion has no barriers. A person's status doesn't define true kindness. Instead, it shows how they see their neighbor with their heart. This parable pushes back on the idea that only those who see themselves as "righteous" can offer mercy. The Samaritan, the one rejected by many, was an example of true love.

The Parable of the Prodigal Son

A young man asked his father for his inheritance and went far away. He spent his inheritance on a life of debauchery, finding himself penniless. He returned home expecting his father to treat him like one of his servants for having spent all the money he had given him. To his surprise, his father welcomed him back with open arms, joyfully celebrating his return.

This story reflects the heart of my heavenly Father. No matter how many mistakes we have made or how far we've strayed, God will always forgive and receive us with love. His mercy is infinite, which is the Gospel's essence. No sin is too great for the grace I offer.

The Parable of the Rich Man and Lazarus

There was a rich man who lived luxuriously, while a poor man named Lazarus lay in misery at his gate. Both died; the rich man went to Hades while Lazarus went to Abraham's side. The rich man, suffering, asked Abraham to send Lazarus to ease his pain. But Abraham said to him, "Between you and us, there is a great gulf." This shows how, in life, our choices matter. The rich man lived for himself while Lazarus lived in humility and faith. Remember, what you do in this life has consequences for eternity.

The Parable of the Ten Virgins

Ten virgins went to wait for the bridegroom. Five of them did not bring enough oil for their lamps. When the groom arrived, he realized some brides were not ready and left them out. This story is a lesson about preparation and vigilance. We should treat the coming of God's Kingdom with great seriousness. Waiting for the Lord requires constant preparation, always being alert and ready. Do not be like the reckless virgins who waited until the last moment to prepare. Spiritual life requires discipline, perseverance, and vigilance.

The Parable of the Talents

This is the story of a man who gave his three servants various sums of money before leaving on a journey. Two of the servants multiplied the sums the master had given them. The third servant, fearful, buried the money and did nothing with it. This story teaches us that there are times when we must take action: don't be afraid to use the gifts God gives us. Don't hide your talents or be afraid to take responsibility for what others have entrusted to you. The Kingdom of God is not for the lazy. It is for those who aspire to live a life of purpose. It teaches us to serve others with what we have. Every person has a mission to fulfill in this world and must do so with commitment.

The Parable of the Sower and the Tares

The Kingdom of Heaven is like a man who sowed good seed in his field, but while he slept, his enemy sowed tares among the wheat. The servants wanted to pull up the tares, but the sower told them not to because doing so would damage the wheat. In the end, the wheat and the tares will be separated at the harvest and the tares will be burned. So it will be at the end of the age: the righteous will be separated from the wicked and the wicked will be thrown into the fire.

The Parable of the Pearl of Great Value

The Kingdom of Heaven is like a merchant looking for fine pearls. When he finds one of great value, he sells everything he has to buy it. That is what the Kingdom of God is like: it is so valuable that we must be willing to sacrifice everything else to obtain it. Nothing in this life is more important than the Kingdom of Heaven.

The Parable of the Workers in the Vineyard

A man hired workers to work in his vineyard during the day. He paid them all the same, regardless of how many hours they had worked. Those who had worked longer complained, but the vineyard owner explained that he had the right to do whatever he wanted with his property and that he should also treat those who had worked less generously. This parable teaches about God's grace. God's Kingdom is not just according to human standards but is a Kingdom of infinite generosity.

Both stories illustrate my message that every soul has immense value before God. In the first story, the shepherd leaves ninety-nine sheep to find one lost sheep. In the second, the father runs to hug his son when he comes back. These stories show God's tireless love for his children. No matter how distant or lost we feel, God's heart always has a place for us.

The Parable of the Great Banquet

A man gave a great banquet and invited many people, but when the time came, everyone made excuses for not coming. The angry host sent his servants to invite the poor, the lame, and the blind to fill his house. So it will be with the Kingdom of God: the first will be last and the last will be first. Whoever does not appreciate the call to his salvation will be left out.

The Parable of the Barren Fig Tree

A man planted a fig tree in his vineyard, but it bore no fruit. After three years, the man asked the gardener to cut it down, but the gardener told him to leave it for another year to fertilize it. If it didn't bear fruit, then it would be cut down. This parable shows God's patience, which gives us time to repent. But that time is not eternal and judgment will come if we don't bear fruit.

The Parable of the Unjust Judge

An unjust judge did not fear God or man. A widow came to him repeatedly for justice. Finally, the judge agreed, saying he did so because the widow bothered him. Will not God bring about justice for His own who cry out to Him day and night? Truly, I say to you, He will, and soon. Do not lose hope, for God hears your prayers.

The Parable of the Mustard Seed

The Kingdom of God is like a small mustard seed that, despite its tiny size, grows into a large tree. It begins in every heart. It may initially seem small, a spark of faith, but nurturing it with prayer, action, and love will allow it to grow into something extraordinary, giving shade and shelter to many. Sometimes, what seems insignificant at first can become something great. Do not underestimate the power of faith, even if it is as tiny as a seed.

The Parable of the Unprofitable Servant

A servant works in the field, and when he returns home, he doesn't expect to be thanked but continues serving. So it is with you: Don't count yourselves worthy of a reward when you have done all the commandments. We are unprofitable servants; we have done what was our duty. Don't seek earthly rewards but heavenly rewards, for whatever you do for my name will be rewarded.

The Parable of the Lost Coin

A woman had ten coins, but she lost one. She lit a lamp, swept the house, and searched until she found it. When she found it, she called her friends and rejoiced. This is the joy in heaven over a sinner who repents. My Father in heaven rejoices greatly when someone turns to Him with a sincere heart.

The Parable of the Lost Sheep

A shepherd has one hundred sheep, but he loses one. The shepherd leaves the ninety-nine sheep and searches for the missing one. This story reflects God's tireless love for each of you. No matter how many are safe, my love does not rest until I find one who is lost. Through this parable, I showed you that, no matter how far you have gone or how lost you feel, I am always willing to seek you out and bring you back. Every soul has infinite value in my eyes. Everyone matters; everyone receives an acknowledgment.

The Parable of the Two Sons

A father asked his two sons to work in his vineyard. The first said he wouldn't, but then changed his mind and went. The second said he would go but didn't. This story shows that it's not words that matter but actions. Many may promise me things, but obedience in their hearts counts. How often we claim we will act is not essential in the Kingdom of God; what counts is our sincerity in actually doing it. Many may promise me things, but obedience in their hearts counts. In the

Kingdom of God, it doesn't matter how often we say we will do something; what matters is whether we do it sincerely.

Each parable I told has a purpose: to awaken in you a deeper awareness of what it means to follow God, live according to His principles, and seek His Kingdom. They are profound lessons on how to live a full life, experience God's unconditional love, and extend that love to others. These parables are still as relevant today as they were centuries ago.

CHAPTER 11

HOW DO I FEEL TODAY?

—— ··●·· ——

Today, I am deeply saddened. My heart is troubled to see how the world has changed, how the love I offered and hoped would multiply has vanished into a fog of indifference, sin, and hopelessness. When you look around, what do you see? Hatred, envy, selfishness, and violence. So many lost souls have forgotten the truth of my message. It pains me to see so many who no longer believe in my Father and have turned away from Him, ignoring my promises and the suffering I endured for them.

The Father has given me a mission that embodies the eternal truth. I return to this world to lead those who believe in me, follow my path to peace and salvation, and fulfill the Father's promise of divine justice. Evil, sin, and injustice have filled this world. I see it daily, in every corner of the earth and in every heart that strays from God. Disbelief has grown, despair has gripped many, and humanity has fallen into an even deeper darkness than in the days before my crucifixion.

In their eagerness to follow their desires, people have lost the ability to see the light that shines in the midst of the darkness. They no longer seek peace but relish in discord. They no longer seek justice but, instead, power. They no longer speak truth but, instead, lies. How could my message of love and sacrifice have endured if those who received my Word had become deaf to it? I feel alone, isolated in a sea of indifference and sin.

My heart fills with sadness as I see how sin has flourished as if people are no longer reluctant to turn away from God. The communities, homes, and hearts of the people all seem empty. Selfishness and materialism have invaded every corner of human life and faith in my Father has been replaced by a false hope in the idols of this world. Greed, hatred, and anger seem to rule hearts and the peace I proclaimed has been lost. Many have chosen to walk in darkness instead of living in the light of love, preferring empty shadows to the truth.

What has happened to compassion? What has happened to forgiveness, the forgiveness I taught? Nowadays, the world is filled with resentment, revenge, and bitterness. Relationships are easily broken, love fades, and the heart's wounds grow deeper. It pains me to see how those who could live in harmony choose conflict; how those who could embrace each other drift away as if the bonds of brotherhood that once united them had become broken.

But what pains me most, what saddens me most, is to see how respect for the mother God gave me has been distorted. My mother! The one who gave me life on this earth, the one who was my refuge, my strength, my example of love and faith. How it pains me to see my mother scorned, rejected, and insulted continuously. It reminds me how many have forgotten her and how they deny and ridicule her! Mary, the one chosen by the Father to be my mother, the one who gave me her unconditional love and suffered with me, was by my side until the very end. She, the one who watched me grow up, the one who saw me preach and accompanied me every step of the way. How great is her pain to see how her son is rejected and how indifference is shown toward her motherhood?

Every child, in their love for their mother, suffers when they see someone insult or reject her. And as her child, I suffer deeply when I see that so many do not honor and respect her. She was my earthly mother and a reflection of God's love on Earth. People have stopped seeing her as the model of humility, obedience, and purity that she was and treat her as if she were any ordinary woman. Her sadness is infinite because, although some may not know it, she continues to pray for you, loves you, and awaits your return to God's love.

But it is not only my mother who is suffering. It is the same God who sent me into the world. The Father, who commanded me to live and die for you, also suffers when He sees so many of His children turning away from Him. And I feel helpless when I see so many reject the sacrifices that I made for them and how they refuse to accept my love. Didn't they see me when I offered myself to them as the Lamb of God? Didn't they see my suffering on the cross? Didn't they understand the message of redemption, love, and forgiveness? Humanity is further from God than ever. And no, I'm not wrong to say this. We live in times when evil has become so common that it no longer seems strange. People have forgotten goodness, justice and truth. As I said in the Scriptures, the world is more corrupt than in the days of Sodom and Gomorrah. Those people who were destroyed by their wickedness were no more sinful than the world is today. The same attitudes of pride, corruption, lust and rejection of the truth are found everywhere. And, just as in those days, modern idols are now rising: money, power, fame, indulgence. These idols are pursued instead of peace, justice, and true love. And I ask you, where is the faith? Where are those who follow me, those who preach hope and peace? Why are so few fighting for justice and working to heal this broken world? I have been given great love to give, but who is receiving it? Nations are turning against one another, families are torn apart, hearts are hardened, and I, who came to teach you to live in peace and love, am still waiting for the world to transform.

Today, I feel deeply sad but also hopeful. Hope has not gone, even though the shadows grow. My heart remains open to those who seek me and want to return to truth and light. My love has not changed; my sacrifice remains. My mother, the one who dedicated her life for me, continues to intercede for you, praying for your return to God's heart.

Even though my heart is filled with sadness today, I never lose hope. I know there is always an opportunity for repentance, conversion and a return to divine love. My mother gave me life and, through her, I give you a new chance to find love and salvation. No matter how far you've strayed, there's always an opportunity to come home.

My sadness today is not only for the indifference and sin that has spread throughout the world but also for the pain of seeing that many still do not understand the message I brought. I sacrificed myself, the bridge between humanity and God, so that they might have eternal life. But many continue to choose darkness over light, selfishness over love. Those who should witness my peace and forgiveness have closed their hearts, which is sad. Humanity has turned its back on me, but I do not stop calling. I do not stop offering the hand of grace, hoping that, one day, all of you will return to me.

It saddens me, yes, but it also angers me to see how my words, my message, are used to justify hatred, division and violence. My message of love has been distorted and manipulated. Those who call themselves my followers have forgotten the foundations of my teaching: love of neighbor, mercy, and forgiveness. My life was a testimony of humility and sacrifice, but many who call themselves my disciples have strayed from that truth. Instead of giving life, they have caused death with their divisions and their condemnations. Instead of being light in the world, they have contributed to the deepening of darkness.

What pains me most is seeing how my sacrifice has not been valued as it should have been. They reject the new life I offer. It pains me to see how many have forgotten my cross, forgotten that it was for you that I suffered and died. I have given my life for all without distinction or limits, but many have returned to their idols and pride. And yet I continue to wait with open arms, hoping that you will return to me one day.

The time has come; the moment many await with longing and others with fear is closer than they think. I, who came to the world centuries ago, returned to help you find the true path, restore your relationship with my Father, and live in peace and love. And now, after having given my life for you, having been rejected and crucified, I speak to you again because my return is imminent.

The Father has given me a mission that, although it may seem distant to some, is the eternal truth. I return to this world, not only to lead those who believe in me and follow my path to a place of peace and salvation but also to fulfill the promise of divine justice. This world has been filled with evil, sin, and injustice. I see it daily, in every corner of the earth, in every heart that strays from God. Disbelief has grown, despair has gripped many, and humanity has fallen into an even deeper darkness than in the days before my sacrifice.

But, as I said before, I did not come only to bring retribution. I came to offer you one more chance, one more space to repent, to turn to me with all your heart. However, the choice is yours. Those who reject my love, who choose sin over grace, will face terrible consequences. My return will bring joy to the righteous and judgment to those who have chosen to remain in darkness. I did not come to bring peace but to bring the truth. And the truth is that those who turn away from my Father and reject salvation will have no part in heavenly glory.

The judgment that will come will be significant because my love and patience are extraordinary. For centuries, I have waited, knocked at the doors of hearts, and given men the freedom to choose. And now, when time is short, when the world has grown dark, judgment will come. There will be no more opportunity for those who have lived in rebellion, sin, and unbelief. Sin cannot be tolerated forever and, when I return, I will see with my own eyes the suffering of those who chose to turn away from the light.

There will be great cataclysms, earthquakes, and heavens that will weep for lost souls. Nations will stagger and humanity will realize that the days of grace have expired. The justice that comes will be like a sword that cuts through all evil. But let not those who follow me fear, those who believe in my name and the name of my Father, for I come to deliver them from the darkness. There will be no more suffering for the righteous. Eternal life will be their reward.

For those who repent and seek my forgiveness there will be a place in the Kingdom of Heaven, a place filled with peace, love, and eternal light. Forgiveness is available to all, but they must repent from the heart, change their ways, and live according to God's will. They must love one another as I have loved them, forgive those who wrong them, and live in justice, humility and peace.

How can they attain eternal heaven? I tell them this: First, they must acknowledge that I am the Son of God, the world's Savior, the only way to the Father. There is no other way by which they can be saved. They must believe in my sacrifice, my death on the cross, and my resurrection because it is through these acts that humanity can be reconciled to God. Second, they must repent of their sins. Repentance is fundamental. They cannot live in sin and expect salvation. Repentance is not only feeling sorrow for the wrong they have done but also changing their hearts and actions. Sin must be forsaken and life in Christ must be embraced.

You must live with faith, with hope, and with love. Love God with all your heart, with all your soul and with all your mind. Love your neighbor as yourself. These are not just pleasant words; it is the true path to eternal life. It is not those who simply say, "Lord, Lord," who will enter the Kingdom of Heaven but those who do the will of my Father. And my

Father's will is that they live in love, in justice, in forgiveness, in peace, and in humility.

Eternal heaven is a place where peace reigns, where there are no more tears, no pain, and no death. It is the place to which I have invited you, and to get there, you must be willing to follow me, to live as I lived; to follow my teachings and to live my love. It is not easy because the path to heaven is narrow, but it is the only true path. Those who choose the broad path of sin and the denial of truth will not enter my Kingdom.

Now, those who persist in their unbelief, those who do not believe in me, those who continue in their sin and do not repent will face terrible consequences. I do not rejoice in saying this, but the truth must be known. If they do not repent before they die, their destiny will be separated from God. The punishment will be great because they have willfully chosen to reject the grace I offered them. There is no hope for those who die in their sin without repenting. I am the way, the truth, and the life. If they do not follow me, they cannot reach the Father. If they choose to ignore my sacrifice and my calling, their path will be eternal suffering, separated from the presence of God.

I do not come to condemn the world but to save it. But judgment is inevitable and my return will be the time to separate the righteous from the unrighteous; those who followed me from those who rejected me. There will be lamentation and weeping for those who do not repent because their destiny will be eternal pain, far from the light and peace of God. I came to offer you salvation, but it is only for those who accept it.

Therefore, I beseech you once again: repent. Return to me before it is too late. There is no time to lose. The Kingdom of God is near and my return will be soon. Heed my call and do not refuse to open your hearts. My love is still waiting; my mercy is still available. No matter how far you have gone, you can always return. My return will be your last chance, but do not wait until the last minute. Come to me now while there is still time and be saved.

My return is near. And my Father sends me to give you justice, to give you peace, to give you eternal life. But I also come to see who has repented, lived in the truth, and followed the path of love. Prepare yourselves because there will be no more opportunity to change when it comes. This is the time of decision; the time of grace; the time of salvation.

CHAPTER 12

MY RETURN

·—·· ●·· —·

As I have already told you, my return will be a momentous event—an event that many will not expect and even fewer will be prepared to receive. My return will not be a brief visit, nor will it be silent or discreet. It will mark the moment of truth, the moment when heaven and Earth meet and humanity will be held accountable for its choices.

I have seen the suffering of this world; I have observed the struggles, the wars, the hunger, the pain, and the despair. Those who follow my teachings have tried to foster peace and love, but those who turned away from me have sown discord. I have offered mercy to those who have sinned and called for repentance, but many have preferred to follow their own path, a path that leads them to the abyss.

I will return with justice, which will cause the separation of the just from the unjust. It is the time for final reconciliation. For those who have followed my path and sought my face with humility and love there will be a reward. You will witness my glory and live in eternal peace. The heavens will open and you will see the Son of Man coming with great power and glory. This is the moment the righteous have longed for. I will see you face to-face and give you what I have always promised: a place in my Kingdom without pain or sadness but with peace, love, and eternal happiness.

My return will also bring judgment for those who rejected me. It will be a terrible time for those who lived in darkness and turned away from the light. I do not come to condemn, but I bring justice. You who have chosen lies over truth, violence over peace, and hatred over love will face punishment for your disobedience. Separation from God will be a matter of location and the state of the soul. You will find yourself cut off from all that is good and pure. It is a sad fate I have tried to avoid for centuries, but the time for mercy is running out.

I want you to understand that my return is not just a matter of justice but love. I have shown my love by giving my life for you and my passion by teaching you the path of forgiveness and redemption. And now I come to offer you once again the opportunity to choose and decide which path you wish to take. The door is open, but it will close at the right time and, at that time, there will be no more choice for those who have rejected grace.

This is why I speak to you today. This is the time to repent, to return to God, to turn away from sin, and to seek holiness. Because when my return comes, there will be no more time. You who still have life can still breathe and have the chance to change and seize that opportunity. Come to me, accept my forgiveness, and follow my example. Do not live in darkness, but walk in the light. My Father awaits you with open arms, as do I.

The Kingdom of Heaven is not just a promise for some future time; it is a reality that begins now in your heart. If you believe in me, accept me as your Savior and live as I taught you, then the Kingdom of God is within you now. The Kingdom's peace, justice, love, and mercy are not limited to what will happen when you return to heaven; you must begin living them daily. Every action you do, every word you speak, every thought you entertain must be in accordance with my will. I'm showing you the path to eternal life.

And to those who still doubt and wonder if all this is real, I say: I am the truth, the way, and the life. No one comes to the Father except through me. There is no other path to salvation. There is no other place where you can find peace and forgiveness except in my presence. I offer you a future without suffering, pain, or death. But you will only achieve that in the future if you repent. Turn to me with a sincere heart and seek the truth with humility.

It will not be an easy path for those who choose to follow me. There will be persecution, there will be difficulties, and there will be moments of doubt. But in those moments, I ask you to remember my words: I am with you always until the end of the age. You need not fear for I have overcome the world. I will give you the strength to face any adversity and, with my Holy Spirit within you, you will be able to withstand everything the enemy puts in your path.

How can the human family attain eternal heaven? I tell you this: First, they must acknowledge that I am the Son of God, the world's Savior, the only way to the Father. They cannot find salvation through any other means. They need to believe in my sacrifice, my death on the cross, and my resurrection. These acts reconcile humanity with God. Second, they must repent of their sins. Repentance is fundamental. They cannot live in sin and expect salvation. Repentance isn't feeling sorry for your mistakes. It means changing your heart and actions too. Forsaking sin is necessary and you must embrace living in Christ.

You must live with faith, with hope, and with love. Love God with all your heart, with all your soul, and with all your mind. Love your neighbor as yourself. These are not just pleasant words. To enter the Kingdom of Heaven, it is not enough to call upon the Lord; you also must do the will of my Father. My Father's will is that they live in love, in justice, in forgiveness, in peace, and in humility.

Eternal heaven is a place where peace reigns, where there are no more tears, no pain, and no death. It is the place I have invited you to enter, and to get there, you must be willing to follow me and live as I lived; to follow my teachings and to live my example of love. It is not easy because the path to heaven is narrow, but it is the only true path. Those who choose the broad road, the path of sin, and the denial of the truth will not enter my Kingdom.

Eternal heaven is for those who persevere in faith; for those who, even when they fall, rise again and again and continue to love even when the world turns its back on them. That is the path to eternal life. It is not an easy path, but it is the only path that leads to true peace. And when you reach that place, come into my Father's presence and see heaven's glory. You will understand that everything you went through here on Earth was worth it. Because at that moment, all the suffering, all the sadness and persecution will vanish in the blink of an eye and you will live forever in the peace and light of God.

So, I say to you, do not lose hope. If you are weary, come to me and you will find rest. If you are lost, come to me and you will find the way. If you feel alone, know that you are never alone. I am your Shepherd and you are my sheep. I will guide you to still waters, feed you with my Word, and protect you with my love. My return will fulfill all the promises I have made to you, but what I desire most is that all of you will be part of that eternal Kingdom.

This is the time of salvation, the time of grace. Wait no longer. Come to me, all those weary and burdened, and I will give you rest. My return will be glorious. I offer you life; I offer you my love; I offer you my peace. All you have to do is accept it. I promise those who do so will receive a warm welcome into my Kingdom, where you will live forever with my Father in heaven.

The punishment that will come will be significant because my love is great and so is my patience. For centuries, I have waited, knocked at the doors of hearts, and given men the freedom to choose. And now, when time is short, when the world has grown dark, judgment will come. There will be no more opportunity for those who have lived in rebellion, sin, and unbelief. Sins can't go on forever and, when I return, I will see with my own eyes the suffering of those who chose to turn away from the light.

There will be great cataclysms, earthquakes, and the heavens will weep for the lost souls. Nations will stagger and humanity will realize that the days of grace are over. The justice that comes will be like a sword that cuts through all evil. But let not those who follow me fear. Those who believe in my name and the name of my Father, for them I come to deliver souls from the darkness. There will be no more suffering for the righteous. Eternal life will be their reward.

Now, those who persist in their unbelief, those who do not believe in me, and those who continue their sins and do not repent will face terrible consequences. I do not rejoice in saying this, but the truth must be known. If they do not repent before they die, their destiny will be to be separated from God. The punishment will be severe because they have willingly chosen to reject the grace I offered them. There is no hope for those who die in their sin without repentance. I am the way, the truth, and the life. If they do not follow me, they cannot reach the Father. If they choose to ignore my sacrifice and my calling, their path will be eternal suffering, separated from the presence of God.

Judgment is, however, inevitable and my return will be the time to separate the righteous from the unrighteous; those who followed me from those who rejected me. There will be mourning and crying for those who do not repent because their destiny will be eternal pain, far from the light and peace of God. I came to offer you salvation, but it is only for those who accept it.

Therefore, I call upon you to repent and return to me before it is too late. There is no time to lose. The Kingdom of God is near and my return will be soon.

Hear my call and do not refuse to open your hearts. My love is still waiting; my mercy is still available. No matter how far you have gone, you can always return. My return will be your last chance, but don't wait until the last minute. Come to me now while there is still time and be saved.

My Father sends me to give you justice, to give you peace, to give you eternal life. But I also see who has repented, lived in the truth, and followed the path of love. Prepare yourselves because there will be no more opportunity to change when I arrive. This is the time of decision—the time of grace and salvation.

CHAPTER 13

THE FULFILLMENT OF GOD'S PROMISES AND JUSTICE

———— ··•●•·· ————

My return will be an act of love and justice. Some expect me to return as a glorious king with great power and majesty; they are not entirely mistaken. But before that glorious moment arrives, there will first be a time of testing for humanity. Evil, which has reigned for so long, will be confronted once and for all. My Father's justice will not allow corruption, violence, and unnecessary suffering to continue. Heaven and Earth will shake because God's judgment will be final. But amid this judgment, there will still be room for mercy.

I do not come to destroy but to save. And so my return will also be an act of redemption for those who still have the opportunity to repent. As long as there is life, there will be hope. My Father has always hoped that His people will repent and return to Him. And as His Son, I come to be the intermediary between you and Him, the bridge that leads you back to eternal life.

For those seeking God's justice their entire lives, my return will be the moment they have longed for. Those who have suffered from evil and those oppressed by the unjust will be comforted. Their suffering has not been in vain. I have seen the tears of those who suffer in silence. People scorn and persecute them for their faith and my name. You will receive the reward of your faithfulness, for I am. My Father sees everything and has promised He will not leave His children forsaken.

But I also want you to know that those who have delighted in wickedness, ignored my call, and preferred riches and power over love and justice will face a dismal fate. I can do no more for those who follow the path of sin.

My love is infinite, but you cannot accept the freedom my Father gave you to choose under coercion. Punishment is not something I desire but something that will come as a natural consequence of your decisions. Disobedience to God must always bring consequences. Sin cannot enter the Kingdom of Heaven because all is pure and holy there.

Upon my return, I will separate the righteous from the unrighteous. The righteous will go to the Kingdom of Heaven, but the unrighteous, those who have continued in their wicked ways, will be cut off from the presence of God. Suffering will be their only destiny because they have chosen not to repent, to reject my mercy, and to remain far from the light.

Even in this sadness, I want to give you one last chance. If you hear my voice and repent, you can still save yourself. But this is the time of decision. Those who reject me today will have no chance in the future to choose again. This is the moment of truth in which you must decide which side you are on: light or darkness.

The Path to Eternal Heaven and Salvation

When I speak of eternal heaven, I describe a place that cannot compare to anything on earth. The Kingdom of God is unlike the kingdoms men have established on Earth. It isn't a land of riches or power but peace and love. Here, peace prevails. When you come to me, I will take away everything that causes you pain. There will be no more crying, suffering, hunger, or death. All of that will be left behind because everything will be perfect in my Kingdom.

But this eternal Kingdom is not just something that comes when you die but something you must begin to experience now. As I have told you, the Kingdom of God is within you. When you decide to follow me and live according to my Word, the Kingdom of God manifests itself in your hearts. There is no room for selfishness, hatred, violence, or resentment. Everything in the Kingdom of God is imbued with love, humility, peace and compassion.

Those who follow my way and my teachings and love their neighbor as themselves will truly enter the Kingdom of Heaven. It doesn't matter how great your sin has been in the past. What matters is that you repent and return to me. If you do this sincerely, you will receive forgiveness because I came to save, not to condemn.

Don't just say you've turned around—show it. Repentance isn't about perfect words or sounding holy. It's a real, messy, honest change of heart. It means letting go of the things pulling you away from me, even if they've been part of you for a long time. It's not enough to say, "I believe." I'm looking for more than lip service. I want to see that belief in your choices, how you treat people and show mercy, patience, and love, especially when it's hard. The love you must show is not only toward those who love you but also toward those who hate you, persecute and harm you. I'm not asking for perfection. I'm asking for sincerity. For a heart that's willing to be changed. That's what following me looks like.

Saying you believe in me isn't enough. I want to see how you live, love, and treat the people around you—the ones who are easy to love and those who aren't. I didn't come to collect words; I came to change hearts.

The Fates of Those Who Repent and Those Who Do Not

If you keep walking in your sin, ignoring the voice that calls you back, the road you're on will only lead you farther from me. This isn't about anger or payback—it's about truth. I offered you a way out, a way home, but I won't force you to take it. If you refuse to turn around, if you won't accept me or walk in the truth I've shown you, then you're choosing a life apart from God. That's what separation is—not some dramatic punishment but the quiet, aching distance of a soul that kept saying no. I came close to that distance. But in the end, you have to want to come back.

The opportunity to repent is present now while there is still time in this life, while you can still hear my voice. But once you reach the end of your life, there will be no more opportunities. Therefore, I urge you to seek my forgiveness while you still can and return to me with all your heart and being. Do not let fear, shame, or pride keep you from drawing near to me. I am waiting for you with open arms. My love for you knows no bounds. But that invitation will only remain open for a time.

My return is near, and when it comes, there will be no more time for regret. Seize now the opportunity to enter the Kingdom of Heaven, to live in the light and to walk in the truth. I am the door; only through me can you enter heaven. Make the decision to follow me today and it will be a decision that will change your life forever.

CHAPTER 14

THE APOCALYPSE AND THE FULFILLMENT OF PROPHECIES

— ••●•• —

I am Jesus and now I will tell you about what is to come: the prophecies I have given to my disciples and those I have revealed in the book, which some call the Apocalypse. The Apocalypse shares a message of revelation.

It shows what will occur at the end of time. I promise you, my Father's words matter. He will fulfill all that He has said. As I have already told you, everything on Earth and in heaven will pass away, but my words will not.

I have come to you with a message of salvation, of mercy, but also with a warning. As you know, the world will come to an end. But the end will not be just destruction but transformation. My Father's divine plan began with the world's creation and will culminate as predicted. Humanity, through its free will, has decided to turn away from the light and will face divine judgment. But humanity also has the opportunity to return to the Father if it repents in time.

My disciples asked me about the end times and I gave them clear signs. What I reveal to you today is not only for those who lived during my time on Earth but for all who live until the end. As I have told you, no one knows when the end will occur, but it will happen as written in the Scriptures.

My Father doesn't send people to hell; they choose it themselves. Please don't wait until it's too late. You don't know when you're going to die. Life in your world is short; life in heaven is eternal.

The Signs of the End Times

The Apocalypse tells us about the signs that will occur at the world's end. It warns us of wars and rumors. It also speaks of famine, plagues, and natural disasters. These signs are just the beginning, but you must not despair. Each event reminds us that time is running out and that my Father's Kingdom is near. When these things happen, lift your head because redemption is near. The world will be plunged into a time of great tribulation, but do not worry if you remain faithful. I have overcome the world and my victory is your victory if you remain steadfast in your faith. Although the forces of evil will rise on Earth and multiply, and the love of many will grow cold, you who follow me must not fear. It is in these dark times that my light will shine the brightest. Persecutors will attack the righteous, but those who persist will find salvation for their souls.

The Antichrist, being evil, will come with promises of peace, but in his heart there is only destruction. He will deceive the nations and many will follow his voice. Signs and wonders will happen. The world will bow to him. But those who belong to my Father and stay true to His Word will not deceive themselves.

The Great Tribulation

The Great Tribulation will be a time of great anguish. No one has ever seen nor will ever see suffering like it. But before that day comes, I will call many to follow me and repent. I will allow them to emerge from that darkness, to return to the Father if they repent of their sins. No matter how dark the world becomes, my light will shine for those who seek the truth. However, many will become hardened in their hearts. The wickedness of men will be evident and faith in my Father will fade in much of the world. Evil will multiply, but those who remain faithful will be those who testify to my name. Do not fear for I will be with you to the end. My Holy Spirit will guide you, comfort you, and protect you.

The Coming of the Final Judgment

Final Judgment will be the moment of truth. There will be no excuses, no deception. Each person's Judgment will depend on their actions, words, and what they did and failed to do. People will judge you by the love you showed, the mercy you gave, and the faith you lived. Also, consider how you treated your neighbor, especially those in need.

The Judgment will be harsh for those who have not repented and those who have lived in sin and rejected mercy. They will face eternal separation from God. It is not a punishment I desire but a natural consequence of their choice because sin, wickedness, and estrangement from my Father separate them from Him forever. The destiny of those who reject salvation is eternal fire. Salvation is a choice each one must make. It's not forced, or not imposed, it is by choice. For those who have followed my path the Judgment will be different. It is not a judgment of condemnation but one of reward. Those who are faithful, love, forgive, and believe in my sacrifice will enter my Father's Kingdom. They will receive eternal life, peace, and joy that knows no end.

The Fall of Babylon

Babylon represents the nations that have turned away from God and who have given themselves over to greed, immorality, and oppression. Babylon symbolizes the world's corruption and its fall is inevitable. Just as ancient Babylon was destroyed, so too will the corrupt system of this world be overthrown. But for those who have stood firm in my Word, there will be freedom, justice, and peace. Do not be afraid when you see corrupt nations and governments fall. My Kingdom is not of this world and is not built on the foundations of wealth, power or oppression. My Kingdom is based on justice, love, peace and truth. When Babylon falls, heaven will rejoice because the triumph of justice will have arrived.

The New Heaven and the New Earth

After the Judgment and the Fall of Babylon, there will be a new heaven and earth. The old creation will pass away and everything will be restored. There will be no more death, no more sadness, no more crying. Everything will be renewed in the perfection of my Father. In this new heaven, there will be no evil or sin. We will be a holy nation, a holy people gathered in the presence of God, living in peace and harmony forever.

This is the promise of hope I bring to you. Although the end will be a time of trials, the restoration that will come will be far more glorious. The gates of heaven will be open to all who have believed and who have persevered in faith. The new Jerusalem will descend from heaven and, with it, the Kingdom of God. It will be a place of eternal happiness where there will be no more pain or suffering.

The Promise of My Return

This is the message I leave with you today. The Apocalypse is not just a book of terror or judgment but a message of hope. It reminds us that evil will not prevail forever and that God's justice will come. Even though many suffer and the world seems lost, I am coming soon to restore all. I am coming to bring the justice you have long awaited. I am coming to gather my flock. I am coming so they may live with my Father in heaven forever.

That is why I give you this message of warning—repent; seek my face; follow my way. I am coming and it will be too late to repent when I arrive. The opportunity is here in the present. Take advantage of this time of grace because the end is near and my return will be like a thief in the night. Be prepared for blessed are those prepared to receive the Lord. This is the end of the revelation. My return will be glorious and everything written in the Apocalypse will be fulfilled.

Therefore, do not be afraid. My peace be with you and my love will guide you to the end. Amen

CHAPTER 15

THE SIGNS OF THE ENDS OF TIMES

———— • •●• • ————

I speak now not with wrath but with sorrow. I speak not to condemn but to call. I offer these words from my heart to yours because the time is getting close and still so many remain asleep. My voice, once heard in the wind, in the whisper of conscience, now cries louder because the days grow darker and my people are walking farther from me than ever before. My return will be a big surprise. Many won't expect it and even fewer will be ready. But this return will not be an occasional visit, as was my first coming when I was born in a manger. This return will not be silent or discreet. It will be the moment of truth. Heaven and Earth will unite and humanity will be responsible for its actions.

There will be wars and also rumors of wars. My child, I told you this to prepare you. The world will grow restless. Kingdoms will clash and fear will grip the hearts of many. You will hear of wars from far away and see the shadow of violence even near your own door. But stay calm. These things must happen before the end. Trust me—I am still on the throne.

False voices will deceive many. There will be those who claim to speak for me, but they do not know me. They will twist my words, promise ease, power, and comfort without the cross. Be watchful. The truth is not always loud, but it is always mine. Stay close to my Word. Know my voice. When you walk with me, no lie can hold you.

Love will grow cold and this wounds me profoundly. The fire of compassion will fade in many hearts. People will care more for themselves than for one another. Even among those who once followed me, bitterness and division will rise. But not you. Let your heart burn with love. You will still remember how I loved you even when the world forgets. I loved with sacrifice and without hesitation.

You will face hatred because of me. You will be misunderstood, mocked, even persecuted—not for doing wrong but for bearing my name. It is hard, I know. But remember, they hated me first. Do not return hate for hate. Bless those who curse you. You are never more like me than when you love your enemies.

Creation itself will cry out. There will be signs in the heavens—strange sights in the skies, trembling on the earth, roaring of the seas. The earth groans, waiting for the day I make all things new. Do not fear these signs; let them remind you that redemption is near. What feels like shaking is only the birth pains of a reborn world.

Many will turn away. It breaks my heart. Some will walk away, not because I failed them but because the cost of following me will seem too great. But I am still here, even for the wanderer. If that's ever you, come back. There is mercy still. I don't turn away those who return to me with open hearts.

The Gospel will reach every nation. No tribe, no tongue, and no group of people will go unnoticed. My message will go to the ends of the earth. I will make myself known through the missionaries, apostles, visionaries, dreams, and visions. I will not return until every ear has heard because I desire none to perish.

Fear will fill the hearts of many. The weight of the world will feel too much to bear. Men's hearts will fail them from terror. But in that moment, look up. I told you—lift your head when these things begin to happen. I am coming. I am not slow. I am merciful. But I will not delay forever. Be strong and courageous.

The days will be like Noah's. People will eat, drink, marry, and live as if nothing will ever change. But the flood came. I'm not saying don't live—I'm saying live awake. Keep watch. Don't let comfort or routine lull you into sleep. The door of the ark is still open, but it will not be open forever.

The world will go through great sorrow—tribulations like never before—but I tell you this so you may have peace in me. I have already overcome the world. You will not be lost if you remain in me and hold fast to my words. Evil will rise. Darkness will spread. Lawlessness will multiply and many hearts will grow cold. Love will be rare. But you, my faithful ones, you must shine all the brighter. My light in you will be a beacon in the chaos.

The ones who endure to the end will save themselves. Not the strongest. Not the loudest. Not the most perfect. But the one who keeps walking with me even when it's hard. Even when it's dark I will never leave you. Hold my hand. Take one step at a time. If you endure, you will see my glory. And I will wipe every tear from your eyes.

When my Father sent you into this world, it was not to chase after the shadows of wealth or build sand empires. It was not to turn brother against brother or use my name as a banner for pride, control, or bloodshed.

You were sent to this world to love, shine like lamps in the night, be salt to the earth, and walk humbly with my Father and me. But what I see now breaks my heart. You have turned away from us.

You, humans, my Father's creation, have filled your hearts with noise and distraction. You chase empty promises in a world that offers everything but delivers nothing. You seek pleasure and forget peace. You lust for power and forget your purpose. You glorify the self and forget the soul. I watch, moment by moment, as the sacred transforms into the profane and the holy faces mockery.

I see churches full of bodies but hearts far from me. I see hands lifted in worship on Sunday and used for violence, corruption, and deceit by Monday. I hear prayers, but I also listen to curses. I hear cries for justice, but few speak for the voiceless. I watch as my cross becomes a symbol of culture, not surrender. You claim my name but not my way. You wear crosses on your neck but not on your back.

I came once, over two thousand years ago, in a manger, lowly, unnoticed by kings, heralded by angels and shepherds. I walked among you. I healed your sick, touched your lepers, wept with the grieving, and fed the hungry. I didn't come to rule but to serve. I didn't come to crush Rome but to crush the chains of sin.

I let you mock me. I let you whip me. I let you pierce me. I bore it all because I loved you that much. And even now, I still do. But love does not ignore truth. And the truth is many of you no longer know me. You know religion. You know sermons. You know theology and ritual. But you do not know my heart. My voice is foreign to you, though I speak. My Spirit knocks, but pride, fear, and distraction lock the door.

You have forgotten why you were sent here in the first place. You were created for eternity, to walk with your Creator, not to chase after temporary highs, likes, and applause. My Father created you to be holy and happy. You were sent to know me. Yet many of you know everything else: trends, fame, news, profits—but not the One who formed you in your mother's womb.

You have immersed yourselves in sin—no longer stumbling into it but diving in headfirst. What once brought shame now brings applause. What once remained hidden in darkness now shines in daylight. You murder the innocent in the name of choice. You mock holy covenant in the name of freedom. You twist my Word to suit your desires. You call evil good and good evil.

Many of you will follow the beast. There will rise an influential leader, a system, a spirit that demands worship and loyalty. Many will bow, even some who once called themselves mine. This call is to integrate and remain firm in the faith. I sealed you with my Spirit, not with the beast's mark. Be alert. The difference may seem small, but the cost is eternal.

And still I wait. I wait for the prodigal to come home. I wait for the thief to look at me on the cross. I wait for the woman at the well to return to the living water. My mercy is still here, flowing like a river. My grace is still enough for the worst of sinners.

I do not desire the death of anyone—I desire repentance, brokenness, and return. But I will not wait forever. The signs are all around you. You hear of wars and also rumors of wars. Nations rise against nations. Creation groans with earthquakes, floods, and fire. The love of many has grown cold. The truth has become a matter of opinion. Self tramples the sacred beneath its weight.

Even the earth knows that the end draws near. These are not threats—they are warnings. I cry out like a shepherd who sees the wolves circling the fold. I call my sheep. I urge them to return to the fold, open their ears, and strengthen what remains before it dies.

The end is not a moment—it is revealing, separating, and reckoning. I do not wish to destroy but will no longer permit the mocking of righteousness. Justice must stand.

To those who still listen, seek me in the quiet places, and still tremble at my Word—I see you. I love you. Hold fast. Do not grow weary. Do not let the darkness around you dim the fire within you.

I am coming soon and my reward is with me; I will wipe every tear, heal the broken hearts, and restore what you lost. But I will also judge what has defied me. My heart is heavy—not with anger but with sorrow. I see a world that has forgotten me; yet I remember every name, every soul, every cry uttered in secret.

I will not forget. I do not sleep. And I do not lie. What I have spoken will come to pass. The end is not the end but a new beginning for those who stay with me until the end.

So I speak from my heart to yours, not with lofty words or hidden mysteries but in a straightforward manner. The time is short. The harvest is ready. The signs are here. Do not delay. Return to me. Let go of your idols. Cast off your pride. Come to me while there is still time.

I have written this so that you may be aware and know that everything written will be fulfilled. My Father's Word is sacred. I also write so that you may prepare and repent of your sins now while you still have time. My hands, my feet, and my side still bear scars. My voice still calls. My Spirit still moves. My love for you is great and I await your change, conversion, and love. But soon the trumpet will sound. And on that day, you will either rejoice or regret.

CHAPTER 16

THE IMPORTANCE OF PRAYER AND THE PURPOSE OF LIFE

— • ● • —

Today, I want to talk to you about a fundamental topic that is often overlooked or misunderstood: prayer and the purpose of life. From the beginning, when my Father created the heavens and the earth, He had a purpose for every human being. Yet many fail to find that purpose or even live without knowing why they were created. You were not created randomly but with a divine purpose intertwined with God's will.

A Link with the Heavenly Father

Prayer is the bridge between heaven and Earth. It is the way your soul connects with the Spirit of God. Many have asked me, "Why pray if God already knows what we need?" The answer is simple: prayer is not just for God to know our desires or needs but for us to know His will so that we may approach Him with humility, trust, and faith. Prayer is an act of surrender, a moment in which we seek guidance from our Creator, acknowledging our dependence on Him.

Prayer is not only asking but also listening. It is dialogue. Just as my Father spoke to the prophets in times past, He also speaks to the hearts of those who approach Him sincerely. In prayer, one can find comfort, strength, direction, and, above all, peace. My life here on Earth was a constant communion with my Father. I prayed in the morning, at night, and in times of difficulty. By praying, one aligns oneself with divine will and one's heart is transformed. Through prayer, we better understand the purpose of our lives.

The Purpose of Life: We Are Not Here by Chance

Now I want to talk to you about the purpose of life, something that many in this world spend their time searching for without finding. I assure you that you have been created with a unique and wonderful purpose. The reason we are in this world is neither an accident nor a mere coincidence. My Father does nothing without a purpose. You are not here simply to live and die. Every life has eternal significance. Life's difficulties, distractions, and worldly worries can sometimes cloud that purpose. Challenges and trials make you wonder, Why am I here? What am I supposed to do?

From the moment of my birth, my life was a fulfillment of divine purpose. Every action I took, every word I said, was part of a more excellent plan. I did not come just to heal the sick or to teach moral lessons; I came to fulfill a much deeper mission: to restore the broken relationship between humanity and God. My sacrifice on the cross, my death and resurrection were the key to opening the way back to the Father's House.

The purpose of each of you is no different. Your life is meant to glorify God, to live in obedience and service. Not everyone has to do the same. Some of you may be called to be pastors, others to be doctors, teachers, or parents. But the essential thing is that all of you must seek, through prayer and faith, the divine purpose for your lives. That purpose may not always be immediately clear; sometimes, it is hidden behind trials and difficulties. However, the purpose is revealed as we trust in my Father and walk in His will.

Confusion and Disenchantment: Why Doesn't Everyone Discover Their Purpose?

There are many who live without understanding why they have been placed in this world. And, yes, it is sad that some never discover their purpose or reject it. This happens for various reasons. Some people are trapped by the world's concerns: money, fame, power, pleasure. These are the false gods that divert attention from what truly matters. Others feel so wounded or trapped in their suffering that they lose hope of finding their purpose. However, I want to tell you this clearly: it's never too late to discover it.

The Path to Self-Discovery

To discover your purpose, you need an open heart. Prayer is the first step. Without prayer, without communication with God, it is difficult to hear the Creator's voice. Remember what I told you: "If you seek, you will find; if you knock, it will be opened to you." This doesn't just refer to prayer for our needs but also prayer for understanding and wisdom. Through prayer, your life aligns with God's purpose. Through prayer, you begin to understand who you are in His plan and what role you play in His Kingdom. I invite you to pray every day, not only with words but also with your heart. Some prayers may be very simple, but their power lies in the sincerity with which you say them.

Here are some prayers to draw closer to God and clarify your life. Prayer is the divine means by which human beings connect with God, the Creator of the universe. During my time on Earth, I taught my disciples and all who listened to me the importance of prayer because I knew that, through it, hearts can draw closer to God and receive the guidance, comfort, and strength that only He can give. Prayer is not just a religious practice; it is a deep and personal relationship with the Heavenly Father, a way to dialogue with Him, express our needs, thank Him for His blessings, and align our will with His.

Prayer is more than a religious practice. It is how we connect with the heart of God, and through it, we discover the purpose for which we were created. Remember that even if you sometimes don't understand everything that happens, God has a perfect plan for each of you. Through prayer, you will be able to know His will and walk toward the eternal purpose He has prepared for you. Do not lose hope for, even if the path is difficult, He is always with you, guiding you toward the life He has planned for you.

Heaven Hear Your Voice

Prayer is a means of direct communication with my Father. It is a space where we can speak to God from the depths of our being. In the quiet of dawn, alone on the hills or deep in the stillness of night, I would pour out my heart to my Father. It's not about perfect words or rituals. It is about being real and honest. I went to Him with everything—hopes, pain, and questions. In those moments, I wasn't just the Son of God; I was a son needing his Father.

Prayer provides a space where nothing will remain hidden and allows you to communicate with my Father. We open a channel of direct communication between us and the Creator. When you pray, be truthful, not hypocritical. Do not pretend to believe what you do not feel to attract attention. When you pray, go into your room, close the door, and pray to My Father, who is in secret. My Father sees you, even in the quiet places where no one else is watching—and He will reward you. Prayer isn't about impressing others. It's a sacred and intimate moment for you and the Father, heart to heart, where no one else needs to see or applaud.

When we pray, a channel of direct communication opens between human beings and the Creator and this is what led me to teach my disciples to pray: "When you pray, do not be like the hypocrites, for they love to pray standing in the synagogues and on the street corners to be seen by others. Truly, I say to you, they have their reward in full. But you, when you pray, go into your room, close your door, and pray to your Father who is in secret, and your Father who sees in secret will reward you" (Matthew 6:5–6). Prayer is not an act to be admired by others but an intimate act between you and God.

Prayer as a Way to Align Our Will with God's

In today's world, human beings often feel lost and confused. Many don't know their purpose or which path they should take. But, through prayer, we find peace in listening to God and understanding His will. When I was on Earth, I taught the people to pray: "Let My Father's Kingdom come. Let Him do His will on Earth, like in heaven."

I taught my disciples and the people of Israel how to pray. I urged them to ask My Father to bring His Kingdom to them. It should be on Earth as it is in heaven. These weren't just words; it was surrender. I understood what it meant to set aside my desires, even when fear shook me. I trusted that my Father's will was stronger. In Gethsemane, I felt the weight of what was coming and still I spoke to my Father. I asked My Father to do His will and not mine.

I want you to know that prayer isn't about convincing God to do things your way. It's about coming close enough to Him that your heart starts to beat in rhythm with His. When you pray with an open heart, you ask for help and let God shape and transform your life. He will lead you into the life He dreamed for you.

Remember that prayer teaches us to submit our lives and desires to God. Through prayer, we ask for His help in our lives. We also open ourselves to His guidance, letting His will take priority over our plans and wishes. Prayer is the vehicle through which our will aligns with God's.

Prayer as a Means of Strengthening Faith

Prayer is also an act that strengthens your faith. When you pray, you know who you are and are not alone. There is someone else, a divine being, who listens to you, cares for you, and knows what you need before you ask.

You can tell a mountain to move even with little faith. It will obey. Nothing will be impossible for you. I'm not talking about physical mountains alone. I'm talking about the significant challenges in your life. These include fear, doubt, pain, shame, and challenging situations that feel stuck. Faith isn't about knowing everything. It's about trusting me. Believe that, with God, even the impossible can happen. It starts small, but even the smallest seed of faith can change everything when placed in my hands.

Faith means believing in God and trusting His power to change your life. Prayer boosts your faith. It helps you feel God's response; through this, you learn to trust Him more.

Prayer as a Source of Peace and Comfort

I know what it means to feel overwhelmed, to face something so heavy that it brings you to your knees. In the Garden of Gethsemane, I felt that weight. I fell to the ground and cried out to my Father, asking Him to take the suffering from me if there was any other way. I was so distressed that my sweat became like drops of blood. But even in that anguish, I surrendered to His will, not because it was easy but because I trusted Him completely. That's where peace came—knowing my Father was near, even in pain. When you pray in tough times, you're not only letting go of your worries, you're also reaching out to the One who holds your life.

Prayer as an Act of Humility and Dependence on God

When you pray, you're acknowledging a truth the world tries to deny: you cannot do life alone. I once told a parable about two men—a religious leader and a tax collector. The leader was proud, convinced of his righteousness. But the tax collector stood at a distance, beating his chest and whispering, "God, have mercy on me, a sinner." It was the humble one who went home justified. Prayer is not about proving your worth but admitting your need. I prayed often because I depended on my Father. You should do the same. Prayer reminds you that God is your strength, source, and guide. Without Him, you feel lost; but with Him, you never feel alone.

Prayer as a Means of Changing Our Hearts

Prayer does more than impact your surroundings. It reshapes your inner thoughts and feelings. I came to show you that the Kingdom of God begins in the heart. I taught my disciples that the pure in heart would see God, but that didn't mean they were perfect. It means they let the Father cleanse them. When you pray with an open heart, bitterness starts to fade. Resentment loses its hold and love can begin to grow. Anger turns to grace through prayer and confusion turns to peace. You refine your soul through prayer. Allow God to work through your prayers. You will experience a transformation of your heart. He will cleanse, heal, and prepare it for His presence.

Prayer as Spiritual Protection

There is real evil in the world and I came face-to-face with it. I battled temptation in the wilderness. I confronted demons and saw how darkness distorts the truth. I taught you to pray, "Deliver us from evil." It was not symbolic but necessary. When you pray, you invite divine protection over your life. You step under the covering of heaven, calling on your Father to defend you against forces you cannot see. Prayer becomes your spiritual armor. It reminds you who you are—children of God—and who stands beside you in every battle. Evil trembles when you pray because you're not fighting alone.

Prayer as an Instrument of Action

Prayer is not only for times of despair or hardship. It is also a means of asking God what you need to serve Him and fulfill your mission in life.

Prayer is essential to the Christian life. You draw closer to God, find peace, and strengthen your faith through it. As I taught my disciples, prayer is a way to express your love for God and align your will with His. You can seek His guidance and support. As you pray with fervor and dedication, you should make prayer a vital part of your daily life. Praying changes your inner world and opens the door to the blessings and divine power God wants to share with you. These prayers will accompany you in spirit and provide comfort and direction. Through prayer, you prepare your heart to love, serve, forgive, and lead. It's where the mission begins.

Prayer as Daily Life

Prayer was never something I did just in a crisis. It was my lifeline. I spoke with my Father often—on mountaintops, in quiet places, even in the middle of chaos. That rhythm of prayer kept me grounded in love and truth. I want the same for you. Let prayer be the heartbeat of your day and don't use it only in emergencies. Instead, keep a constant conversation with God. When you speak with Him often, you open your life to His voice, comfort, and power. That's how you stay connected to what matters most. That's how heaven enters your daily routine.

Prayers for Difficult Times

When the pain is too much and the answers aren't clear, remember this: my Father hears every word you say. I know what it's like to be in agony, weep, question, and hope. That's why I've given you these prayers—not as rituals but as lifelines. They are your way of holding on when everything is falling apart. These prayers will carry your heart into the presence of God. In them, you'll find strength to endure, clarity for your next step, and peace to trust what you can't yet understand. You are not alone. He is with you, even in the silence.

You don't need to read or learn complicated prayers. Talk to my Father as if you were talking to a friend. Tell him what's happening to you; he'll listen. Ask for his help; he'll never leave you alone if you do it with faith. My Father and I are here when you need us. Remember that my Father said nobody will go to heaven unless it comes through me.

CHAPTER 17

PRAYER FOR DIFFERENT OCCASIONS

—— · · ●· · ——

Prayers support and accompany you through different moments and strengthen your faith and relationship with God. Don't forget that He always hears our prayers. When you pray, do it with great faith and you will see the results. Faith moves mountains. Prayer opens the door that leads us to eternal life, to be with God forever.

Remember that your purpose is not limited to being in this life alone. There is a promise beyond this world, an eternal Kingdom where you will live in the presence of God. Stay strong in faith, pray for His will, and turn from sin. Then you will inherit God's Kingdom. Prayer opens the door to heaven. This life is our true purpose: to be with God forever.

I didn't write these prayers because I had all the answers—I wrote them because we needed them. I was guided by Jesus, sometimes through whispers, sometimes through silence, but always through love. These prayers came from real places in my life—moments of fear, hope, surrender, and trust. I hope they meet you where you are, just like God met me. I've learned that something shifts when you speak to Him with honesty and faith. He listens. And if you keep showing up with your whole heart, you will feel Him closer than you ever imagined.

The Prayer of the Sincere Heart

————— ··•·· —————

My Father, in the name of Jesus, I thank You for giving me life and this day.
I ask You to guide me and help me know the purpose for which You created me.
Help me to live each day according to Your will, to be faithful, and to trust in You.
Open my heart so that I may hear Your voice. In your hands, I place my worries and my life.
Amen.

Prayer of Repentance

———— ··●·· ————

God, I acknowledge that I have sinned.

I've wandered far from what You've wanted for me and carried things I should've laid down long ago. I'm tired of pretending, tired of running.

I need Your forgiveness—not just for the things I've done but for the ways I've doubted You, ignored You, and tried to do life on my own. I give You what's left of me.

Please take it. Change me from the inside out.

Make me new. I want to live the life You dreamed for me before I took my first breath.

I don't deserve it, but I trust that Your mercy is bigger than my failure. I'm Yours.

Amen.

Prayer for Wisdom and Understanding

—— ··●·· ——

Lord, You are wise and know everything.

I ask You to give me wisdom and understanding so I may walk in Your will.

Help me discern Your purpose for my life and not be distracted by the things of the world. Give me clarity and strength to do Your will.

Amen.

Prayer for Inner Peace

— · ·•· · —

Lord, in this moment of silence, I ask You to fill me with Your peace.

Calm my mind and heart and help me find serenity amid difficulties.

May Your peace, which surpasses all understanding, govern my life.

Amen.

Prayer for Strength and Courage

————— ··●·· —————

Lord, give me the strength to face the challenges of each day.

Help me be courageous and not fear the future, knowing that You are always with me. Renew my spirit so that I may always move forward in faith.

Amen.

Prayer for Wisdom in Decisions

———— ··•·· ————

Lord, when I must make decisions, enlighten my mind with Your wisdom.

Guide me on the right path and give me discernment to choose what pleases Your heart.

May I always seek Your will in everything I do.

Amen.

Prayer for Forgiveness

—— ··●·· ——

Lord, I ask You to help me forgive those who have offended me, as You have forgiven me. Release me from anger and bitterness.

Fill my heart with Your love.

Amen.

Prayer for the Sick

———— ··●·· ————

Lord, I pray for all who are suffering from physical, mental, or spiritual illness.

Fill them with Your healing and comfort.

Place Your healing hand upon them and give them strength in their struggle.

Amen.

A Prayer for Peace in My Home

————— ··•·· —————

God, I'm tired of the noise, the walls that echo with silence or shouting—please bring Your calm here.

Let every room in this house breathe out the weight we've carried and take in something softer, something whole.

Help us to hear each other again, not just words but the ache beneath them.

Let love be louder than pride and forgiveness faster than anger.

If peace is a light, even a flicker, show us how to guard it like fire in the cold.

Stay with us, stay in us—until this house feels like a happy home again.

Amen.

A Prayer for Steady Belief

—— ··●·· ——

God, I'm worn and unsure, but I still want to believe—help me hold on when everything in me is ready to let go.

My faith flickers like a candle in the wind and I need Your breath to keep it alive.

I don't need perfection, just enough trust to take the next step, even if I can't see the road.

Remind me that doubt doesn't mean I've failed You—it means I'm still reaching.

Let Your love break through the noise of my fear and settle like a quiet truth in my bones.

I'm Yours, even when I'm trembling—carry me when I forget how to walk in faith.

Amen.

A Prayer for Discernment in a World of Deception

————— ··•·· —————

Lord, I can't always tell who speaks the truth and who wears a mask.

So please open my eyes before my heart goes astray.

Give me a hunger for Your voice so deep that no imitation can satisfy it.

When smooth words and grand signs try to pull me in, remind me that even wolves can dress like shepherds.

I'm not wise on my own—teach me to test every spirit, to cling to Your Word more than anyone's promises.

Protect my soul from the kind of lies that sound holy but lead to ruin.

Keep me close to You, even when the world twists Your name for its gain.

Amen.

Prayer to the Holy Spirit for Guidance and Right Decisions

·•●•·

Holy Spirit, I'm facing choices that feel too heavy for me and I don't trust my understanding.

Whisper Your wisdom into the noise of my thoughts and show me which way leads to life.

I've made wrong turns, chasing comfort or approval, but I want to follow You this time.

If the path is hard but holy, give me the courage to take it anyway.

Shut every door that pulls me away from God and flood my heart with peace when I walk in Your will.

Don't let fear or pride be louder than Your quiet voice inside me.

Lead me not to an answer but to You because You are the one I'm searching for.

Amen.

A Prayer for Health in Body and Spirit

———— ··●·· ————

God, I'm tired of feeling weak, worn down, and uncertain about what's happening inside me.

Please reach into my body and bring healing.

You know every cell, every ache, every fear.

I don't speak out loud and I need you now more than ever. I'm not asking for strength to get through the day—I'm asking for wholeness from the inside out.

If healing takes time, give me patience; if it comes through doctors, guide their hands and minds.

When I wake up afraid of what the day might bring, meet me there with Your calm.

Heal more than my symptoms—heal the worry, frustration, and loneliness of sickness. Let me have steady breath, strong steps, and hope anchored in You.

Even if the healing isn't instant, help me trust that You're with me through it all.

Amen.

A Prayer for My Family

———— ··●·· ————

Lord, You gave me this family—not perfect, not easy, but deeply mine—and I lift them to You with open hands.

Cover them with Your protection, especially in the places I can't reach and the battles I can't see.

Bring peace to tense moments.

Heal those in pain.

Spread laughter where silence lingers.

Teach us to forgive with haste, speak kindly, and hold one another with grace.

When life pulls us in different directions, be the center that holds us together.

Help me love them not just in words but in patience, sacrifice, and prayer.

Strengthen the tired, calm the anxious, and bring home the ones who feel far, even if they're right beside us.

Thank You for every heartbeat we've shared—help us grow in love, even in the mess of it all.

Amen.

A Prayer to Hold My Family Close

———— ··•·· ————

*God, I come to You with a heart full of love and worry for my family—
please hold them in Your hands when I cannot.*

*You see the pain we try to hide, the tension behind our smiles, and the
love that sometimes gets lost in the noise.*

*Please give us the strength to carry one another when we're too tired to
stand.*

*Help us speak truth without hurting and listen with hearts that don't
rush to judge.*

*Heal the wounds we've caused by silence or shouting and teach us how
to forgive with open arms.*

*Let joy revisit our home, not only in the good times but even in the
struggles.*

Guide our choices, protect our bodies, and calm our restless minds.

*When distance, anger, or life gets in the way, pull us back to one
another and You. Make our home where love is louder than fear and
grace is never in short supply.*

*Thank you for the gift of each person I call family—help me love them
like You do. Amen.*

MYRA LOPEZ

A Prayer for Peace

———— ··●·· ————

God, this world is falling apart—drowned in anger, fear, and deep sorrow.

We don't ask for silence that conceals our hurt.

We yearn for real peace that heals the damage within people and nations.

Help us see one another not with doubt or distance but as Your children.

We all carry Your breath.

Let justice rise like a mighty flood, sweeping away the selfishness and cruelty that crush the vulnerable.

Let justice roll like a river, washing away the pride and power that trample the weak. Give courage to peacemakers, wisdom to leaders, and compassion to those with the loudest voices.

Hold the suffering close and remind the violent that love is stronger than any weapon.

Help us forgive what seems unforgivable and hope when the world gives us every reason not to.

May Your peace not just visit this world but live in it and grow through us.

Quiet the noise of anger that drowns out empathy.

Replace every bitter seed with mercy that can bloom.

Help us to hear each other again, not just words but the ache beneath them.

Let love rise above our pride, and let forgiveness come quicker than the heat of our anger.

If peace is a fragile flame, teach us to shield it—like hands cupped around fire in a winter wind.

Please don't leave us.

Remain with us, dwell within us—until these broken walls become holy ground, and this house becomes home again.

Amen.

Prayer before bed

------- ··•●•·· -------

God, as I lay down tonight, I bring You my tired heart.

The day was heavy in places I didn't expect, and I didn't have all the answers.

But You see me, even in silence. Calm my racing thoughts. Heal what hurts inside. Forgive where I've fallen short, and help me let go of what I can't fix. Wrap me in Your peace and remind me that I am not alone—not in this room or life.

Stay with me through the night. Speak to me in my sleep.

And if I wake, let it be with hope.

Amen.

Prayer thanking God

— ··•·· —

God,

Thank you—for everything I forgot to thank you for. For breath in my lungs and strength to stand, even when the weight of life feels like too much.

Thank you for the quiet moments, the unexpected kindness, and the grace I didn't earn but needed more than I knew.

Thank you for holding me together when I felt falling apart.

There were days I doubted, nights I cried, and hours I felt lost—but You never left.

You stayed, even in my silence, even in my stubbornness.

Thank You for Your patience, for seeing beauty in my mess, for calling me worthy when I couldn't see it myself.

Thank you for those who love me, the tough lessons that helped me grow, and every small light You've put in dark spots.

Thank you for loving me—not only when I'm faithful but also when I'm flawed and forgetful.

I don't say it enough, but I'm grateful.

You've given me more than I asked for, more than I deserve, and more than I often realize.

So tonight, I express my gratitude to You with complete sincerity.

With all I am.

Amen.

EPILOGUE

LETTER FROM JESUS

——— ·•●•· ———

My beloved children,

I am writing this message with the utmost urgency. A message that comes from my broken heart. You have the proof from when I was on Earth. You know all I went through. You saw my mother's pain as she watched me die on the cross. Still, you won't believe it. Many welcomed me, but more turned away. They chose the comfort of darkness instead of the call to the light. My father, a God of love, has given you many opportunities to reach heaven, but you have rejected them.

I gave everything—my breath, body, blood—for a world that spat in my face even as I saved it. I stood in for you. I took on your shame. I endured the nails, not from duty but from a love deeper than you can imagine. And yet, the very people I came to rescue have turned their hearts away. You sing about me, speak my name, but your lives are far from me. My cross has become a decoration; my words background noise. I see a world that once shouted, "Hosanna!" and now mocks me with its idols, pride, and apathy. Do you know what it feels like to be forgotten by the ones you died for? To be betrayed by the souls you held so close? It breaks me—not because I am weak but because my love is real. Love always feels the wound deeper.

You have become like the Egyptians, bowing to false gods of gold, pleasure, power, and self. Statues may not stand on your streets but you have given your hearts to gods that cannot speak, save, or love.

These things you chase are empty, yet you worship them as if they gave you life. But there is only one God, the Maker of heaven and Earth— my Father. I came to show you His heart. I came to bring you home to Him. And still you run. Still, you fill your souls with noise, hoping to drown out the silence where my voice used to be. But I am still here. Wounded, yes. Rejected, yes. But waiting, with the same love that once stretched out its arms on a cross for you.

Now I speak in simple terms—time is running out. The door of grace remains open but will not stay open forever. My return is near, not as the Lamb but as the Righteous Judge. Not to plead but to reckon. I will come in glory, not hidden in a manger but with fire in my eyes and truth on my tongue. Every heart will reveal itself. No title, no excuse, no mask will shield you from the light of what is true. But still I'll call you. Come out of the shadows. Let go of your bitterness, your pride, your shame. It's not too late. But justice will come and, with it, the world as you know it will pass away. To those who have suffered, waited, and endured, their redemption draws near. To those who have lived as if I never existed, your moment of decision is now. Not tomorrow. Not someday. Now.

I do not say these things to alarm you but to awaken you. There is light eternally shining and it is I. I have always been here. I am not distant. I am the truth you've searched for in every wrong place. I am the peace behind every restless night. I am the beginning and I will be the end. Choose me. Choose eternal life with the Father. Amen.

I Am,

Jesus of Nazareth

The end is near. This world has little time left. However, my Father's love is infinite. He is willing to welcome all who repent. Do not let the passing shadows of this life cause you to lose your soul. The temporal will soon fade, but life is eternal and full of peace and love in heaven. Come before the door closes; salvation is near, and my arms are open.

My soul weeps with sadness to see how many of you will lose your souls and be damned. And when that happens, you will burn in hell because hell exists. You will repent, but you will no longer have the chance. You will live there forever.